Nick Vandome

Windows 11 for Seniors

in easy steps

2nd edition

for PCs, Laptops, and Touch devices

In easy steps is an imprint of In Easy Steps Limited
16 Hamilton Terrace · Holly Walk · Leamington Spa
Warwickshire · United Kingdom · CV32 4LY
www.ineasysteps.com

Second Edition

In Easy Steps Limited supports The Forest Stewardship
Council (FSC), the leading international forest
certification organization. All our titles that are printed
on Greenpeace approved FSC certified paper carry the
FSC logo.

MIX
Paper from
responsible sources
FSC® C020837

Printed and bound in the United Kingdom

ISBN 978-1-78791-022-5

Contents

1 Getting Windows 11

This chapter explains how Windows 11 has evolved, identifies the new features, and shows what's needed to upgrade your existing computer. It also details how to create a Microsoft Account.

About Windows 11

Windows 11 is the latest release of Microsoft Windows, the operating system for personal computers. There has been a long list of Windows releases, including:

- 1995   Windows 95
- 1998   Windows 98
- 2000   Windows Me
- 2001   Windows XP
- 2003   Windows XP MCE
- 2007   Windows Vista
- 2009   Windows 7
- 2012   Windows 8
- 2013   Windows 8.1
- 2015   Windows 10
- 2021   Windows 11

When you buy a new computer, it is usually shipped with the latest available release of Windows. This takes advantage of the hardware features generally available at the time. Each year sees new and more powerful features being incorporated into the latest computers. In line with this, the requirements for Microsoft Windows have increased steadily. For example, the minimum and recommended amounts of system memory have increased from 4 megabytes (MB)-8MB in Windows 95 to 1 gigabyte (GB)-4GB in Windows 11. There's a similar progression in terms of the processor power, the video graphics facilities and the hard disk storage requirement.

This means that your computer may need upgrading or extending in order to use a later release of Windows, especially if you want to take advantage of new capabilities such as touch gestures. To take full advantage of new features, you may need a new computer.

Each release enhances existing features and adds new facilities. Thus, the latest Windows 11 is able to support all the functions of Windows 10 and prior releases, along with enhancements, plus its own unique new features. These allow you to carry out tasks that might not have been supported with previous releases of the operating system.

Within each Microsoft Windows release there are several editions catering for different types of users, such as Home, Pro and Enterprise.

Windows 11 has received significant annual upgrades since it was introduced in 2021. The latest is the Windows 11 2024 Update, which is the version used for this book.

Which Release is Installed?

To check which release of Windows is currently installed on your system, you can look at the **System** panel, which is located in the **Settings** app. This can be accessed in different ways.

- Press the **WinKey** + **Pause** key in any version of Windows to display the **System** panel.

- Click on the **Settings** app on the Taskbar (if it has been pinned there; see page 36) at the bottom of the screen and click on the **System** option in the left-hand panel and the **About** option.

- Right-click on the **Start** button on the Taskbar and click on the **System** option.

WinKey is another name for the **Windows logo** key. The **Pause** key is labeled Pause/Break.

For all three methods, the operating system details will be shown (along with user, memory and processor information). This includes the version of Windows being used, listed under **Windows specifications** > **Version**.

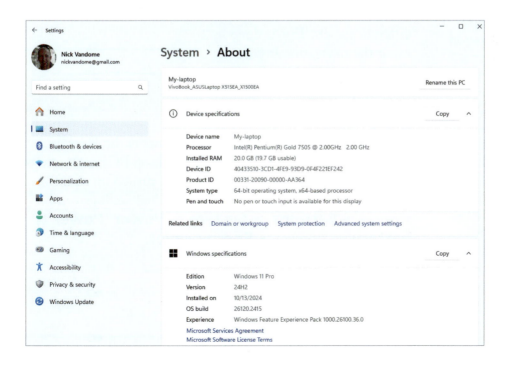

New Features of Windows 11

Copilot

The main innovation in the Windows 11 2024 Update is an overhaul of Copilot, the digital assistant that is powered by Artificial Intelligence (AI). Introduced in 2023, Copilot is now a standalone app that appears as an icon on the Taskbar. It can be resized and moved around the screen, and also pinned to the Start menu and the Taskbar in the same way as any other app. The Copilot app can be used to answer a huge range of voice and text queries by harnessing the power of AI and the internet.

Teams and chat

These features are new or updated in the Windows 11 2024 Update. These new features are available on all devices that can run the Windows 11 2024 Update.

The Teams app now incorporates the chat function, which was previously included as a separate app. This means that text and video chats can be made directly from the Teams app.

Quick Settings

The Quick Settings panel has been updated so that you can move through all of the options without having to access different panels. This is done by using the navigation buttons at the right-hand side of the Quick Settings panel.

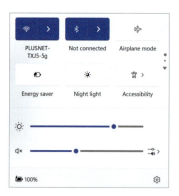

Energy Saver

A new option in the Quick Settings panel is the Energy Saver function. This can be used on desktop PCs and laptops to reduce power consumption. It can be turned on or off in the Quick Settings panel, and its individual settings can be accessed in **Settings** > **System** > **Power** (**Power & battery** on laptops) > **Energy saver**.

On some of the most recent Windows 11 devices using the Snapdragon X processor, there is a function known as Windows Recall. This captures screenshots of your current screen every five seconds and stores them locally on your computer. These screenshots can then be used to retrace your steps of whatever you have been working on. However, this feature is not available on all Windows 11 devices.

What's Needed

The minimum configuration recommended by Microsoft to install and run Windows 11 is as follows:

- **Processor**   64-bit, 1GHz or faster.

- **System memory**   4GB or larger.

- **System firmware** Unified Extensible Firmware Interface (UEFI)- and Secure Boot-capable.

- **Security**   Trusted Platform Module (TPM) 2.0 encryption device.

- **Graphics card**   DirectX 12 devices or later with Windows Display Driver Model (WDDM) 2.0 driver.

- **Storage**   64GB or larger.

- **Display**   High-definition (720p), 9" diagonal or greater, with 8 bits per color channel.

There may be additional requirements for some features; for example:

- Internet access for online services and features such as Windows Update.

- Five-point touch hardware for touch functions.

- A network and multiple PCs running Windows 11 for file and printer sharing.

- An optical drive with rewriter function for DVD/CD authoring and backup function (and for installation of Windows 11 if provided on DVD).

- Audio output (headphones or speakers) for music and sound in the Media Player.

If you are not able to upgrade your existing PC to Windows 11 and are not ready to switch to a new device, Windows 10 will continue to be supported until October 2025.

The terms "32-bit" and "64-bit" relate to the way the processor handles memory. You'll also see the terms "x86" and "x64" used for 32-bit and 64-bit respectively.

The product functions and the graphics capabilities may vary depending on the system configuration.

Microsoft PC Manager

Keeping a Windows 11 PC running smoothly is essential to getting the best out of the operating system. One way this can be achieved is with the Microsoft PC Manager app, which has a range of options for monitoring your computer and boosting its performance. To use it:

1 Enter "Microsoft PC Manager" into the Search box on the Taskbar and click on the **Install on Windows** button

2 The app is displayed in the Microsoft Store. Click on the **Get** button

3 Click on the **Open** button to open the app from the Microsoft Store, or

4 Click on the **PC Manager** option on the Start menu

The Microsoft PC Manager app can also be accessed directly from the Microsoft Store by clicking on the app below on the Taskbar or the Start menu and then using the Search box to locate the app. The app may not currently be available in all locations.

5 Click on the **Start** button to begin using the PC Manager app

6 The left-hand sidebar contains the main categories within the app. Click on one to view the options in the main panel. For instance, click on the **Home** button (if it is not already displayed) to view the most common options within the app

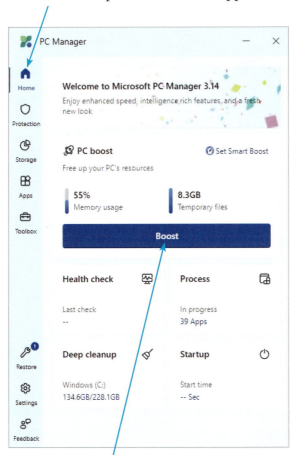

Hot tip

Click on the **Settings** button in the left-hand sidebar to access options for how the PC Manager app operates.

15

7 Click on the **Boost** button to improve the overall performance of your computer. As the process is undertaken, a rocket icon appears on the button

...cont'd

8 Click on the **Protection** button in the left-hand sidebar to view security options, such as performing a virus scan and managing pop-up windows

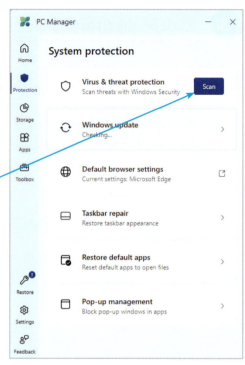

The **Deep cleanup** option in Step 9 can also be accessed from the **Home** section.

9 Click on the **Storage** button in the left-hand sidebar to view options for optimizing storage on your computer, using the **Deep cleanup** option

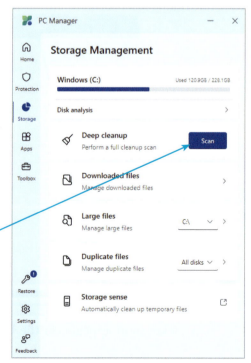

...cont'd

10 Click on the **Apps** button in the left-hand sidebar to view details about installed apps and also **Uninstall apps**, as required

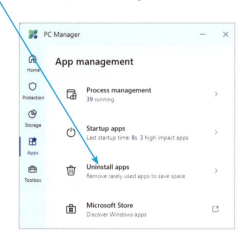

11 Click on the **Toolbox** button in the left-hand sidebar to view general options for **Windows tools** and **Web tools**

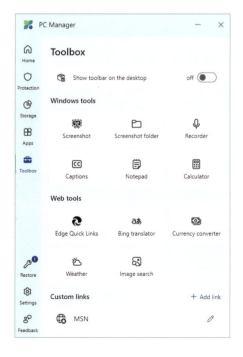

17

Drag the **Show toolbar on the desktop** button **On** in Step 11 to display the PC Manager toolbar in a floating panel that sits above whatever is on the screen.

Installing Windows

Windows 11 is primarily an online service rather than just a standalone operating system. This means that by default, Windows 11 is obtained and downloaded online, with subsequent updates and upgrades also provided online on a regular basis.

The main ways of installing Windows 11 are:

A Microsoft Account is needed to synchronize settings and access the Microsoft Store to download apps and updates. You can create a Microsoft Account from **Accounts** in the **Settings** app (see Chapter 4).

- **Windows Update** – Replace an older version of Windows, retaining the installed apps and settings. This can be done through the **Settings** app (select **Windows Update** and click on the **Check for updates** button).

- **Microsoft website** – Visit the software download page on the Microsoft website (**microsoft.com/en-us/software-download/windows11**) to use the **Windows 11 Installation Assistant** to download Windows 11.

- **Pre-installed** – Buy a new PC or laptop with Windows 11 already installed.

- Microsoft has also made a DVD available to install Windows 11 directly rather than via additional updates.

Some of the steps that the installation will go through are:

- **Personalize**. These are settings that will be applied to your version of Windows 11. These settings can also be selected within the **Settings** app once Windows 11 has been installed.

When there is already a PC associated with your Microsoft Account, you can choose to copy Windows apps and settings from that PC or set up your system as a new PC.

- **Settings**. You can choose to have express settings applied or customize them.

- **Microsoft Account**. You can set up a Microsoft Account during installation or once you have started Windows 11.

- **Privacy**. Certain privacy settings can be applied during the setup process for Windows 11.

Keyboard Shortcuts

As you become more confident using Windows 11, you may want to access certain items more quickly. There are a range of keyboard shortcuts that can be used to access some of the items you use most frequently.

The majority of shortcuts are accessed together with the **WinKey** (Windows key) on the keyboard.

You can change the image that is displayed on the Lock screen and even provide your own image (see page 73 for details).

To use the keyboard shortcuts, press:

- **WinKey** to access the Start menu at any time.

- **WinKey** + **L** to lock the computer and display the Lock screen.

- **WinKey** + **I** to access the Settings app.

- **WinKey** + **K** to connect new devices.

- **WinKey** + **Q** to access the Search window.

- **WinKey** + **D** to access the desktop.

- **WinKey** + **M** to access the desktop with the active window minimized.

- **WinKey** + **E** to access File Explorer, displaying the Home folder (if this has been specified).

- **WinKey** + **T** to display thumbnails on the desktop Taskbar.

- **WinKey** + **U** to access the Accessibility options in the Settings app.

- **WinKey** + **X** to access the Power User menu, which gives you quick access to items including the desktop and File Explorer.

- **Alt** + **F4** to close a Windows 11 app, or close Windows 11 from the desktop.

- **Ctrl** + **Shift** + **Esc** to access Task Manager.

Using a Microsoft Account

A Microsoft Account is required to get the most out of Windows 11 and many of its functions. This is a registration system (which can be set up with most email addresses and a password) that provides access to a number of services via the Windows 11 apps. These include:

- **Outlook**. This is the Windows 11 app that covers email (**Mail**), address book (People) and calendar (**Calendar**).

- **Teams**. This is the collaboration and communication app, including the chat function that can be used for text and video messaging.

- **Microsoft Store**. This is the online store for previewing and downloading additional apps.

- **OneDrive**. This is Microsoft's online backup and sharing service that can be used with a Microsoft Account and Windows 11.

Creating a Microsoft Account

It is free to create a Microsoft Account. This can be done with an email address and, together with a password, provides a unique identifier for logging in to your Microsoft Account and the related apps. There are several ways in which you can create and set up a Microsoft Account:

- During the initial setup process when you install Windows 11. You will be asked if you want to create a Microsoft Account at this point. If you do not, you can always do so at a later time.

- When you first open an app that requires access to a Microsoft Account. When you do this, you will be prompted to create a new account.

- From the **Accounts** section of the **Settings** app (see page 69).

Without a Microsoft Account you will not be able to access the full functionality of the apps listed here.

Whichever way you use to create a Microsoft Account, the process is similar.

1 When you are first prompted to sign in with a Microsoft Account you can enter your account details, if you have one, or

2 Click on the **No account? Create one!** link

Hot tip

Microsoft Account details can also be used as your sign-in for Windows 11.

21

3 Enter your name, an email address and a password (on the next screen) for your Microsoft Account

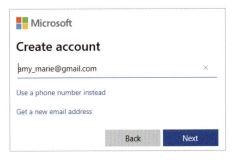

4 Click on the **Next** button to move through the registration process

Next

5 A verification code is required to finish setting up the Microsoft Account. This will be sent to the email address entered in Step 3. Click on the **Next** button to complete the Microsoft Account setup

Hot tip

See pages 164-166 for details of how to verify your Microsoft Account.

Closing Windows 11

When you finish working with Windows, you'll want to shut down or sign out. Here are three ways to do this:

Hot tip

If supported by your hardware, you are offered the option to put the PC to sleep. You'd use **Sleep** when you're going to be away from your PC for a while. It uses very little power, and when you return and touch the screen or move the mouse, the PC starts up quickly, and you're back to where you left off.

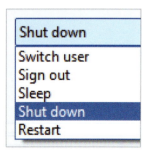

Don't forget

In Step 3, click the **Down** arrow to display all of the shut down/restart options.

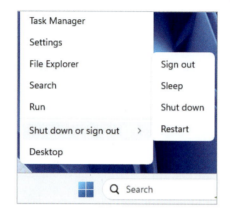

1 Right-click the **Start** button (or press **WinKey + X**) and select **Shut down or sign out**, then choose the particular option that you require; e.g.
> **Sign out**
> **Sleep**
> **Shut down**
> **Restart**

2 On the Start menu, click the **Power** button to select **Sleep** (if offered), **Shut down** or **Restart**

3 From the desktop you can also press **Alt + F4** to display the **Shut down** option

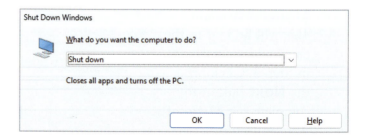

2 Windows 11 Interface

Windows 11 offers an updated interface, with a clean design featuring subtle shades and a centralized Start button and Start menu.

This chapter shows how to get started with the latest version of Windows, including details of using apps with Windows 11.

Starting Windows 11

Switch on your computer to start up the operating system. The stages are as follows:

1 A simple Windows logo is displayed, with a rotating cursor to show that the system is being loaded

2 After a while, the **Lock** screen is displayed

The startup time depends on the configuration of your computer and how it was previously closed down, but usually it is less than a minute.

3 Press any key, click a mouse button, or swipe up on a touchscreen monitor to display the user **Sign in** screen

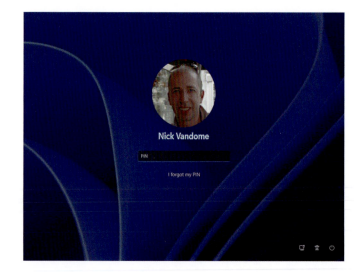

Windows remembers the last sign-in option used and presents that option the next time you sign in with that account.

24

4 Use the sign-in option and press the **Enter** key (in this example it is a PIN number)

5 The Windows 11 desktop screen is displayed, showing the background associated with your account

Multiple user accounts

If there are multiple user accounts, you can select the required account to sign in with the relevant details.

If there is more than one user account, the **Sign in** screen will display the last used account, along with a list of available accounts. For more details about working with user accounts, see pages 82-85.

Start Button and Start Menu

When you start Windows, you can see the apps that are provided. These vary depending on the edition of Windows installed.

1 From the **Lock** screen, sign in using your PIN code to display the desktop

Nick Vandome
I forgot my PIN

Don't forget

Windows systems start up on the desktop, and you can display the Start menu using the **WinKey** or the **Start** button.

2 On the desktop, click the **Start** button to the left of the Taskbar icons (or press or tap the **WinKey**)

3 The Windows **Start** menu displays, showing the **Search bar**, **Pinned** apps (see page 36), **Recommended** files and a button for **All** apps

4 Click the **All** button in Step 3 on the previous page to see your apps and an alphabetic list of all your apps

Don't forget

Entries with a folder icon expand when you click them and contain groups of items – for example:

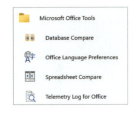

5 Move the mouse pointer to the right of the Start menu to display the scroll bar

Hot tip

At the bottom of the Start menu is the active user account. Click this to change its settings or to select a different user account.

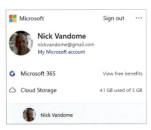

6 Scroll down to view the other items that are to be found in your **All** list

...cont'd

7 On the **All** screen, click on one of the alphabetic headings; e.g. C

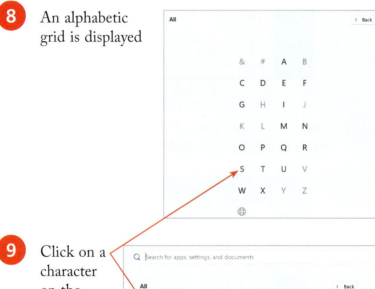

Hot tip

Use the Search box at the top of the Start menu to search for specific apps.

8 An alphabetic grid is displayed

9 Click on a character on the alphabetic grid to go to the relevant section

Repositioning the Start Button

Although the **Start** button has moved into a more central position, along with the Taskbar, it is still possible to restore it to the left-hand corner if desired. This is done by moving the whole Taskbar to the left. To do this:

1 Click on the **Settings** app on the Taskbar or the **Start** menu

2 Click on the **Personalization** tab

3 Click on the **Taskbar** option

4 Click on the **Taskbar behaviors** option

5 Click here in the **Taskbar alignment** panel to select options for how the Taskbar is aligned

6 Click on the **Left** option to align the Taskbar to the left-hand side, situating the **Start** button in the left-hand corner

In Step 6, all of the icons on the Taskbar are aligned to the left, in addition to the **Start** button.

Power User Menu

There's a menu of useful shortcuts associated with the **Start** button (on the left of the Taskbar icons).

1 Right-click the **Start** button to display the **Power User** menu

2 Alternatively, press **WinKey** + **X** to display that same menu

This allows you to access a set of functions that are often needed by a more advanced user, which include the System panel, Device Manager, Disk Management, Terminal, Task Manager, Settings, and Run.

Select the **Shut down or sign out** option, and you can choose to sign out, sleep, shut down or restart your system.

Make sure that it's the **Start** button that you right-click, or you'll get the right-click action associated with the alternative area you click. On the desktop (for example), you would get the Screen menu with View, Sort by, Refresh, etc.

Right-click the Taskbar, and you get the option to open **Taskbar settings**.

This opens **Settings** at the **Personalization** option, with Taskbar selected so that you can adjust the Taskbar properties.

1 Show or hide the Taskbar buttons:
Search
Task view
Widgets

2 For the **System tray icons** option, choose items, as required

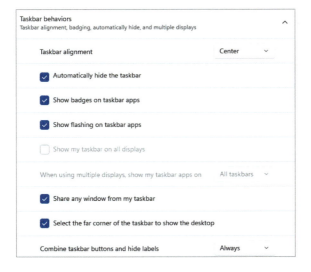

3 Click on the arrowhead next to the **Other system tray icons** options

4 Drag the buttons **On** or **Off** to choose which icons may appear in the system tray

Scroll down to the **Taskbar behaviors** section, where you can select the setting for Taskbar alignment or choose the **Automatically hide the Taskbar** option, when you move the mouse pointer away from the Taskbar area.

You can also choose **Show badges on taskbar apps** and **Show flashing on taskbar apps**.

The system tray is the collection of icons at the right-hand side of the Taskbar.

Click the **Up** arrow (^) on the Taskbar to reveal the contents of the Taskbar corner overflow area.

A badge on a Taskbar app is a small icon symbol on the app's icon that indicates if there are notifications or updates for the app.

Desktop Layout

Both tablet and standard PCs start with the desktop screen. This is similar to the display from earlier versions of Windows, with desktop icons, and the Taskbar with **Start** button, shortcuts and active apps, Quick Settings and the date and time. Here, you see a Classic app and two Universal apps running in windows on the desktop:

Desktop icons   Universal apps   Classic app   Background

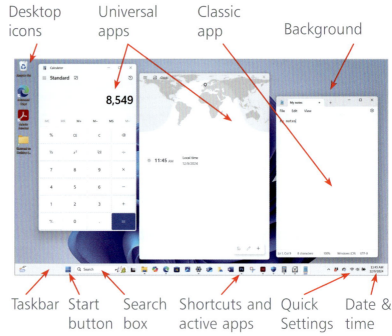

Taskbar   Start button   Search box   Shortcuts and active apps   Quick Settings   Date & time

When you left-click the **Network** icon or the **Volume** icon on the right-hand side of the Taskbar (or press **WinKey** + **A**), you will display the **Quick Settings** flyout.

Left-click the date and time (or press **WinKey** + **N**) to display a flyout bar on the right of the screen. This displays the **Notifications area**, beneath which is a panel for creating Focus sessions for when you do not want to be disturbed – see page 72.

Click the **Start** button to display the **Start** menu: a merger of the features of the Start menu and the Start screen from previous versions of Windows.

Pinned apps

Recommended section

All button

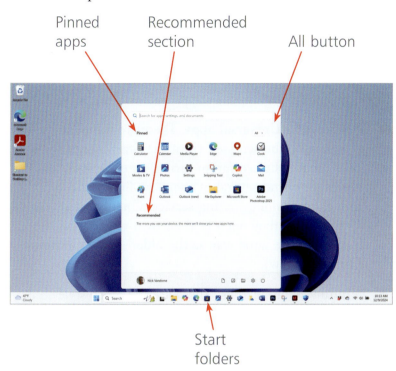

Start folders

To close the Start menu and redisplay the desktop, click the **Start** button, click anywhere on the screen outside the Start menu, or press the **WinKey**.

33

1 Scroll the **All** list to see the full set of apps on your system

2 Right-click the **File Explorer** icon on the Taskbar to get links to the desktop and to specific parts of the file system, including **Downloads**, **Documents**, and **Pictures**, and also to list your frequently accessed files

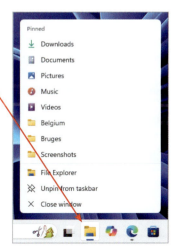

To close the folder list, left-click anywhere on the screen away from the folder list itself.

Hot tip

Windows 11 Universal apps are so named because they can be used on a range of devices running Windows 11, including tablets and touchscreen computers. They are generally newer apps than the older Windows Classic apps. They will be referred to as Universal apps throughout the book, unless otherwise stated.

Using Apps with Windows 11

The word "app" is now firmly established as a generic term for computer programs on a range of devices. Originally, apps were items that were downloaded to smartphones and tablet computers. However, the terminology has now been expanded to cover any computer program. So, in Windows 11, most programs are referred to as "apps", although some legacy ones may still be referred to as "programs".

There are three main types of apps within Windows 11:

- **Windows 11 Universal apps**. These are the built-in apps that can be accessed from the Start menu. They cover the areas of communication, entertainment, and information, and several of them are linked together through the online sharing service, OneDrive. In Windows 11, they open in their own window on the desktop, in the same way as the older-style Windows apps (see below).

- **Windows Classic apps**. These are the older-style Windows apps that people may be familiar with from previous versions of Windows. These open in the desktop environment.

- **Microsoft Store apps**. These are apps that can be downloaded from the online Microsoft Store, and cover a wide range of subjects and functionality. Some Microsoft Store apps are free, while others have to be paid for.

Windows 11 Universal apps

Windows 11 apps are accessed from the icons on the **Start** menu. Click on an icon to open the relevant app.

Windows Classic apps

Windows Classic apps are generally the ones that appeared as default with previous versions of Windows, and would have been accessed from the **Start** button.

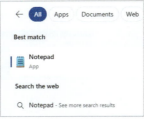

Windows Classic apps can be accessed from the Start menu by using the alphabetic list or searched for via the Taskbar Search box. Windows Classic apps have the traditional Windows look and functionality, and they also open on the desktop.

Microsoft Store apps

Microsoft Store apps are accessed and downloaded from the online Microsoft Store. Apps can be browsed and searched for in the Store, and when they are downloaded they are added to the **All** alphabetic list on the Start menu.

The Microsoft Store is accessed by clicking on the **Microsoft Store** tile on the Start menu or on the Taskbar.

Apps can be pinned to the Start menu, or the Taskbar, by right-clicking on them in the All list of apps and selecting either **Pin to Start** or **More > Pin to taskbar**. To unpin a pinned app, right-click on it on the Start menu, or the Taskbar, and select **Unpin from Start** or **Unpin from taskbar**.

With a Windows 11 touchscreen or tablet, tap the tile to start the app. With the keyboard, navigate to the required tile using the arrow keys and then press **Enter**.

Opening an App

Universal and Classic apps may be found as icons on the Taskbar and the **Pinned** section of the Start menu, or alphabetically in the **All** list.

1 To open an app, move the mouse pointer over one of the entries for the desired app – **Weather**, for example – and left-click to open it

2 The app opens full-screen or windowed, depending on how it was last loaded, with weather details for the default location

3 Switch back to the **Start** menu to choose another app – **Maps**, for example

4 The app opens, again either full-screen or windowed, overlaying the previous app

5 Load more apps as required, which all appear overlaid on the desktop, with the most recent one appearing at the top

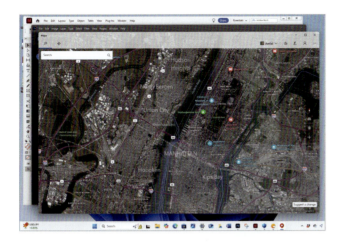

Don't forget

Individual apps may be shown full-screen or windowed. You can follow the same procedures in either case.

When you have several apps running, you can show all active apps and choose one to work with next.

1 Click the **Task View** button (or press **WinKey + Tab**) to show all the apps, and click on one

Don't forget

You can organize your apps on several desktops, keeping related apps together – for example, a work desktop and a gaming desktop. See pages 50-51 to set up a new desktop.

2 Alternatively, hold down the **Alt** key and tap the **Tab** key until the app you want is selected, then release **Alt**

Arranging App Windows

You can arrange your active apps manually by dragging them into the required positions, which is known as **Snap Assist**.

1 Start with several apps open, as windows on the desktop or as full-screen

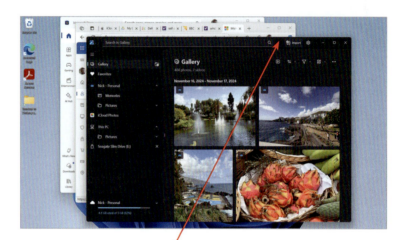

2 Click the **Title bar** on one app and drag it to the side of the screen, then release the mouse button when a frame appears showing the new location

Don't forget

You can select an app and press **WinKey + Left** arrow or **WinKey + Right** arrow to split the screen, then select a second app for the other half.

3 The other apps are displayed in Task View style on the other half of the screen. Select an app to be displayed in that half

Click and drag the edges of a windowed app to resize it on the screen.

With two apps displayed side by side, click and drag the edge between them to widen one window and narrow the other.

39

4 To arrange four apps on the screen, click on the **Title bar** of each app in turn and drag it to a corner

You can position apps in corners using the keyboard. Press **WinKey** + **Left** arrow then **Up** arrow for the upper-left corner. For the other corners, use the (**Right**, **Up**), (**Left**, **Down**) and (**Right**, **Down**) combinations.

If you have a dual-monitor system, you can have sets of two or more apps displayed on each monitor.

Snap Layouts has been updated in the Windows 11 2024 Update.

Don't click on the button in Step 1 as this will maximize the window.

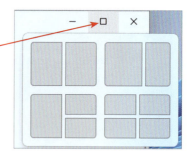

Not all third-party apps support the Snap Layouts feature.

Snap Layouts

Windows 11 provides great flexibility when it comes to working with windows: it is possible to display up to four active windows at a time. This is known at Snap Layouts, which can be accessed from the control buttons at the top of any window. To use Snap Layouts:

1 Open an app and move the cursor over this button in the top right-hand corner of the window. This displays the Snap Layouts panel

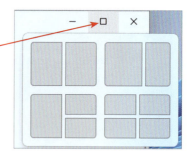

2 Click on one of the thumbnails in the Snap Layouts panel

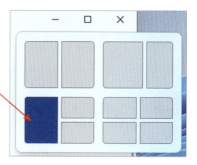

3 The app is displayed in the position selected in Step 2

4 If there are other open apps, they will be displayed as thumbnails in one of the available Snap Layouts panel. Click on one of the thumbnails to maximize the selected app in the panel

Apps can be rearranged once they have been assigned a position in a Snap Layout by accessing the Snap Layout as in Step 1 on the previous page and selecting a new location for the app.

5 Open another app and repeat the process in Steps 1 and 2 to position it as required

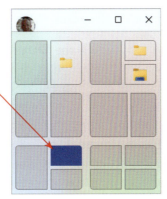

Apps can be "unsnapped" from their positions by clicking and holding on the Title bar and dragging them into a new position.

6 The app is displayed in the position selected in Step 5

Display Resolution

To check the active resolution of your PC monitor:

1 Right-click the **Start** button and select **Settings**, then select **System** > **Display**

2 Scroll down to **Display resolution** where the display resolution is specified

You can also right-click a clear portion of the desktop and select **Display settings** from the list presented.

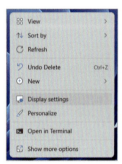

3 Click the **Down** arrow to show the range of display resolutions that you could apply

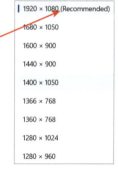

The best setting is marked **Recommended** and is the native and highest setting for your monitor. This is the setting that you should use in most situations.

If you select a lower resolution you'll be asked to specify whether you want to keep these display settings.

1 Click **Keep changes** to apply the new setting, or select **Revert** to cancel the change

If you make no response, a countdown proceeds and, after 15 seconds, the display resolution automatically returns to its previous value.

Closing Apps

When apps are running in windowed mode, they feature the **Title bar** with its **Close** button.

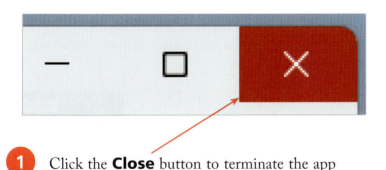

1   Click the **Close** button to terminate the app

When the app is running full-screen, it continues to display its Title bar so that you are still able to end the app by clicking its **Close** button.

You can also close an app by switching to that app and then pressing **Alt** + **F4**. Alternatively, with the app selected, press **Alt** + **Spacebar**. This displays the **Title bar** menu. Click on **Close** to close the app.

From the Taskbar, right-click the app icon and select **Close all windows**. This will immediately close all active instances of that app.

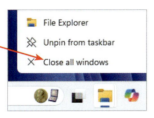

Alternatively, move the mouse pointer over the app icon until an app thumbnail appears, then click its **Close** button.

This method allows you to close a single instance of an app when there are multiple copies active.

Hot tip

Apps not being displayed run in the background (if supported) or get suspended. This lets them restart quickly. However, you may prefer to explicitly close unwanted apps.

Don't forget

If you have problems closing a specific app, you can always run **Task Manager** by right-clicking on the **Start** button and selecting the **Task Manager** option. Once **Task Manager** is open, right-click on the app that is causing problems and select the **End task** option.

43

Searching with Windows 11

Windows 11 has a Search box built in to the Taskbar. Separate searches can be performed with Copilot, the AI digital assistant (see pages 46-48).

Using the Search box for text searching

To use the Search box for text-only searches, over either your computer or the web:

1 The Search box is located to the right-hand side of the Start button. At the right-hand side of the Search box is an image that relates to particular events specific to the current day or just of general interest. Move the cursor over the image to view details about it

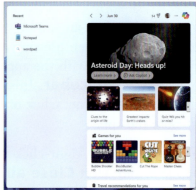

2 Click on the Search box image to expand the Search panel and view more details relating to the Search box image

3 Click in the Search box and enter a search term (or website address)

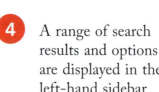

4 A range of search results and options are displayed in the left-hand sidebar

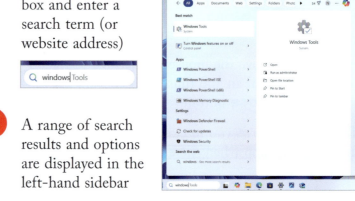

It is possible to turn off the Search box image so that it does not appear. To do this, access the Search settings as shown on the next page, scroll down the page to **Show search highlights** and drag the button **Off**.

44

Hot tip

5 Click on the categories on the top toolbar to view different search result options for the query; e.g. **Apps**

Search settings

To access the settings for the Search facility in Windows 11:

1 Click on the menu button at the right-hand side of the top toolbar in the Search results panel and select **Search settings**

2 Apply the Search settings as required, including the **SafeSearch** options for the type of content that can be shown in search results

3 Scroll down the page to view more Search settings, including those relating to how your search history is used and viewed. This can be in terms of your search history on the device being used and also any history stored in the cloud

Hot tip

If you are searching for a keyword in the Document category in Step 5, the search will be conducted over the text in documents and folders on your computer, not just the document titles. It will also search over the online backup and storage facility, OneDrive, if you have this set up (see page 118).

45

Hot tip

Click on the **Privacy dashboard** link below the **Search history in the cloud** heading to open a web page where you can manage your data and privacy settings from your Microsoft Account.

Copilot has been updated in the Windows 11 2024 Update.

Copilot replaces the Cortana search functions that were available in some previous versions of Windows.

Copilot

Artificial Intelligence (AI) is the latest buzz phrase in the world of computing, and it is indeed both artificial and intelligent. However, in terms of everyday computing, AI is not as intimidating to use as it perhaps first seems: in many cases, AI is part of the apps on a device, and users may not even be aware of its existence. In Windows 11, the Copilot app is an example of how AI is incorporated into the functionality of the operating system. It is a digital assistant powered by AI that can understand natural language requests (written or spoken), analyze data, and provide detailed responses based on an extensive range of collated information. To get started with Copilot with Windows 11:

1 Click on this button on the Taskbar

2 Click in the query box toward the bottom of the screen to start a text query conversation

3 Enter a question into the query box and click on this button

4 An answer to the query is provided by Copilot; in this example, an extensive recipe

5 If required, scroll down the page to see the full answer from Copilot

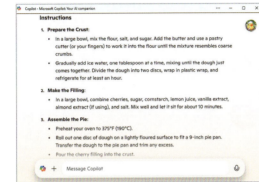

6 A new search query can be made at any point, as part of the current conversation (see the second tip)

7 The reply to the new query continues as part of the same conversation; in this example, the reply is in the form of a bulleted list

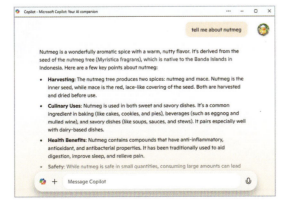

Click on the microphone icon at the right-hand side of the Copilot query box to make a voice query rather than a text one.

Click on the **+** button at the left-hand side of the Copilot query box and click on the **Start new chat** option to start a new conversation, as opposed to a new query within an existing conversation.

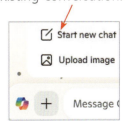

...cont'd

Searching with photos

One way in which Copilot uses its intelligence is by being able to identify photos and provide information about them. This can be done from a photo already on your device or one that is taken by the device. To do this:

1 Click on the **+** button at the left-hand side of the Copilot query box and click on the **Upload image** option

2 Navigate to the image to be used and select it

3 The selected image is added in the query box. Enter text, as required, and click on this button

4 Information about the selected image is displayed by Copilot

If Copilot cannot identify a location in a photo, it will just give a general description.

3 Windows 11 Desktop

This chapter shows how Windows 11 still supports the traditional windowed desktop environment, including the Taskbar, Notifications area, and the familiar window structure and menus.

New Desktops with Task View

A useful feature in Windows 11 is the Task View option. This is located on the Taskbar and can be used to view all open apps and also add new desktops. To use Task View:

1 Click on this button on the Taskbar

2 Task View displays minimized versions of currently open apps and windows

Don't forget

Apps can only be open on one desktop at a time. So, if an app is open on one desktop and you try to open it on another, you will be taken to the desktop with the already open app. For adding desktops, see the next page.

3 As more windows are opened, the format is arranged accordingly

Don't forget

Although the shortcuts and background are the same for each desktop, the Taskbar will change depending on the open apps.

4 If an app has more than one window open (e.g. File Explorer), each window is displayed within Task View

5 Click on a window in Task View to make it the active window

Adding desktops

Another function within Task View is for creating additional desktops. This can be useful if you want to separate different categories of tasks on your computer. To create additional desktops:

1 Click on the **Task View** button on the Taskbar

2 The current desktop is displayed

3 Click on the **New desktop** option

4 The new desktop is displayed on the Task View window. Click on the new desktop to access it. Each desktop has the same background and shortcuts

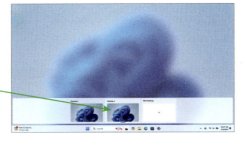

5 Open apps on the new desktop. These will be separate from the apps on any other desktop

Beware

If you add too many desktops it may become confusing in terms of the content on each one.

Hot tip

To delete a desktop, click on the Task View button and click on the cross that appears when you hover your mouse over the desktop you want to remove.

51

Hot tip

Press **WinKey** + **Ctrl** + **D** to create a new desktop and then switch to it immediately.

Don't forget

Click on the **Task View** button to move between desktops.

Taskbar

The contents of the Taskbar change dynamically to reflect the activities that are taking place on your desktop.

As more apps are opened, they appear on the Taskbar.

52

Taskbar shortcuts

At the left of the Taskbar is the **Start** button (the Windows logo button). To the right of this are the **Search**, the **Task View** and the app buttons – **File Explorer**, **Copilot**, **Microsoft Edge**, and the **Microsoft Store**. These are apps provided by Microsoft. You can also pin your own choice of apps here. The app icons turn into task buttons when you run the apps.

Task buttons

There is a task button for each active task, above. The selected task – in this case, **Microsoft Store** – will be shown with a full underscore. An active but not selected task, such as the **Microsoft Edge** browser, has a shorter underscore. There is no underscore shown for apps that are not open, as with **Copilot** in this example.

Notifications area

On the right of the Taskbar is the **Notifications area**, with the system icons, including **Network**, **Speaker**, and **Battery** (for a laptop or tablet) buttons and date and time values.

Search box

Click in the **Search** box, to the right of the Start button, to look for apps, documents, web pages, and more (emails, folders, etc.) and open the main Search panel.

Hot tip

The date and time, which is displayed at the right-hand side of the Notifications area, can be edited in **Settings** > **Time & language** > **Date & time**.

53

Hidden icons

Click on the ^ symbol, at the right-hand side of the Taskbar, to show hidden icons.

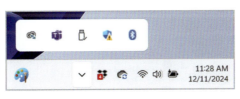

54

Notifications

To make sure that you are aware of notifications as they become available:

1 Click the **Settings** button on the Taskbar if it has been pinned there (see page 36), or open Settings using the Start button (see page 11)

Don't forget

You can choose to turn notifications **On** or **Off** for specific apps and other senders.

2 On the **System** panel that is displayed, scroll down to select **Notifications**

3 Ensure that the **Get notifications from apps and other senders** option is turned **On**

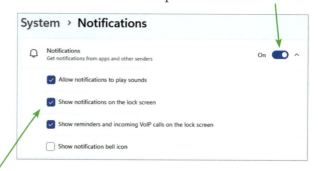

You can choose from **Allow notifications to play sounds**, **Show notifications on the lock screen**, **Show reminders and incoming VoIP calls on the lock screen**, and **Show notification bell icon**

Don't forget

Scroll down and expand **Additional settings** to request suggestions and tips on setting up your device and on using Windows, or select **Get help** to contact Microsoft Support.

Show Desktop

When you have several apps running, their windows will obscure the actual desktop.

The **Win** + **D** key combination also performs **Show desktop** operations. Press once to reveal the desktop. Press again to restore the windows.

1 Hover the mouse pointer over the far right of the Taskbar to reveal the **Show desktop** button, a narrow vertical line

If the **Show desktop** button isn't displayed, you can enable it in **Settings** > **Personalization** > **Taskbar** > **Taskbar behaviors**.

2 Click the **Show desktop** button to hide the windows and show only the desktop and its icons

Click the **Show desktop** button a second time to redisplay the app windows.

Widgets

The Widgets panel in Windows 11 contains a number of real-time items, such as newsfeeds and weather forecasts, that change as new information becomes available. Items in the Widgets panel are fully customizable. To use the Widgets panel:

1 Click on this icon in the left-hand corner of the Taskbar (if this icon is not visible, go to **Settings > Personalization > Taskbar**, and for **Taskbar items**, drag the **Widgets** button **On**)

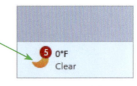

2 The Widgets panel is displayed, with the default widgets. Click on a widget to display more comprehensive information about the item (opens in the Edge browser)

3 Scroll down the page to view the rest of the available widgets and their content

4 Move the cursor over a widget and click on this button in the top right-hand corner to close (hide) a widget

Adding channels

Channels covering specific categories of information can be added to the Widgets panel, and these will display regularly updated content, relevant to the channel heading. To add channels:

1 Click on the **Account** button in the top right-hand corner of the Widgets panel to open the **Personalize Microsoft Start** panel. Click on the **Discover** tab to view channels that can be added to your feed

Click on the **Following** tab at the top of the Widgets panel (or the panel in Step 1) to view the channels that you have selected to follow and options for adding more channels.

2 Scroll down the page to view more channel options. Click on the **+** button next to a topic to add that channel of information to the Widgets panel

...cont'd

Adding widgets

To add individual widgets to the Widgets panel:

1 Click on the **Add widgets (+)** button next to the **Widgets** heading

2 The left-hand panel contains categories that can be included. Click on a category to view its widgets

Hot tip

To remove a widget from the Widgets panel that has been added with the details on this page, click on the menu button in the top right-hand corner of the widget and click on the **Unpin widget** option.

3 Click on the **Pin** button underneath a widget to add it to the Widgets panel

Working with widgets

Options for individual widgets can be accessed from the widget in the Widgets panel, and general settings can also be used.

1 To access options for a widget, move the cursor over the widget and click on this menu button

2 Select options for the widget as required (these may vary depending on the type of widget)

- Fahrenheit
  Celsius

  🐵 Hide this widget
  ✏ Customize widget
  ✩ Pin widget

Hot tip

For some widgets, the menu button on a widget provides options for pinning items to the Widgets panel or blocking them. The latter is a good way to remove content in which you are not interested.

⊕ Follow Newsweek
⊘ Block Newsweek
✩ Manage interests

↪ Share
⑦ Why am I seeing this?
⚑ Report an issue

Widget settings

To access a range of settings for the Widgets panel:

1 Click on this icon in the top right-hand corner of the Widgets panel

2 Select options for settings for the Widgets panel, including **Discover new widgets**, **Personalize**, and **Notifications** to be sent notifications when content in a widget is updated

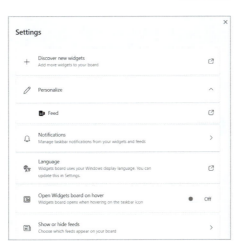

Settings ✕

+ Discover new widgets
  Add more widgets to your board

✏ Personalize ^

   📰 Feed

🔔 Notifications
   Manage taskbar notifications from your widgets and feeds

🌐 Language
   Widgets board uses your Windows display language. You can update this in Settings.

Open Widgets board on hover   ● Off
   Widgets board opens when hovering on the taskbar icon

Show or hide feeds
   Choose which feeds appear on your board

Desktop Icons

Shortcuts to any Windows app can be stored on the desktop. To start with, there are standard system icons.

You can change desktop icons from the default size (**Medium**) to **Large**, as shown here, or to **Small**. You can also change their size by pressing the **Ctrl** key and scrolling the mouse wheel, to vary between very small and very large.

60

1 To display or resize icons on the desktop, right-click an empty part of the desktop and select **View**

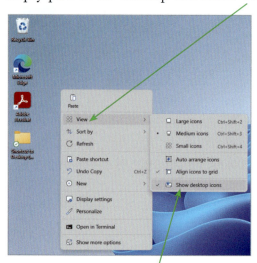

2 If the **Show desktop icons** entry is not already selected (checked), then click to enable it

3 Select **Personalize** from the right-click menu, and choose **Themes > Desktop icon settings**

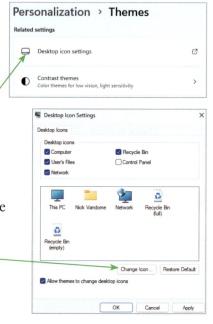

4 Select icons that you wish to display, then click **OK** to apply the changes

Click the **Change Icon...** button in Step 4 to select alternative images for any of the system icons. Click **Restore Default** to revert to the original images.

For quick access, you can add shortcuts to the Taskbar for both Classic and Universal apps.

1 Find an app in the **All** section of the **Start** menu

2 Right-click on the app and click on the **More** > **Pin to taskbar** option

You can now run the app from the Taskbar. However, if you prefer, you can create an app shortcut on the desktop, where there's room for lots of app shortcuts. To do this:

1 Right-click on the desktop and select **New** > **Shortcut**

2 Navigate to the location of the required app, select it, and click on the **Next** button

3 Enter a name for the shortcut, to be displayed on the desktop, and click on the **Finish** button

4 The shortcut is displayed on the desktop. Double-click on it to open the app

You can right-click the Taskbar icon for any app that has been pinned there and select **Unpin from taskbar** to unpin the app from the Taskbar.

Apps are usually located in the **Program Files** folder on the **C:** drive.

Shortcuts on the desktop can be pinned to the **Start** menu by right-clicking on them and selecting **Pin to Start**.

...cont'd

You can also create shortcuts on the desktop using drag and drop from the **All** list, for both Classic and Universal apps.

1 Scroll to an app in the **All** list, such as the **Calculator** app

2 Select and drag the app icon onto the desktop, and release it when a **Link** flag appears

3 Similarly, scroll to another app such as **Weather**, and drag and drop it onto the desktop

You can add other apps, such as **Word** and **Excel** from the **Microsoft 365** suite (if you have subscribed to the Microsoft 365 suite or have purchased these apps), and apps such as **Maps**.

You can drag the desktop shortcut icons to arrange them in groups according to type, perhaps, or by project or activity. If you have many icons on your desktop, you can group them in folders (see page 80) to make them easier to locate.

Window Structure

When you open a folder, or start a Windows function or app on the desktop, it appears as a window that can be moved and resized. For example:

1 Click the **Paint** icon found in the **All** list on the **Start** menu

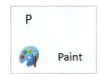

See page 64 for Notepad, an example of a simpler window.

Features of an app window (Paint)

Title bar   Menu bar   Minimize and Maximize   Close button

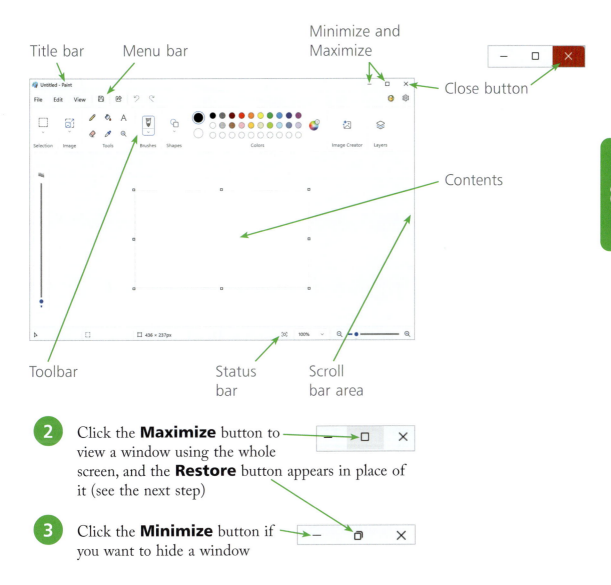

Contents

Toolbar   Status bar   Scroll bar area

63

2 Click the **Maximize** button to view a window using the whole screen, and the **Restore** button appears in place of it (see the next step)

3 Click the **Minimize** button if you want to hide a window

App Windows

Even in Windows 11, apps may still use the traditional window structure, with a **Title bar** and a **Menu bar**. For example, see the **Notepad** app:

1 Select **Start** > **All** > **Notepad**

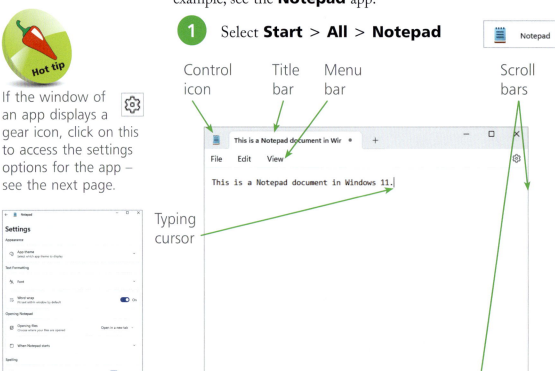

Control icon

Title bar

Menu bar

Scroll bars

Typing cursor

Hot tip

If the window of an app displays a gear icon, click on this to access the settings options for the app – see the next page.

Some Windows apps, such as Word in the Microsoft 365 suite of apps, use the Scenic Ribbon (Ribbon) for accessing the functionality of the app. See pages 142-145 for more details about using Word and Microsoft 365.

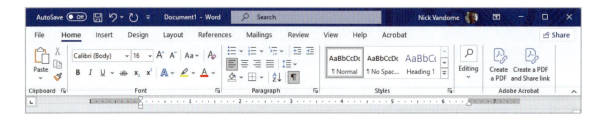

Menus and Dialog Boxes

Menu bars are the rows of textual headings at the top of many apps. If they are clicked on, they provide a list of related options to choose from. Some entries expand into a sub-menu; for example:

Open Notepad from **All** and click **View** on the Menu bar to display the options, then hover over **Zoom** to display its subset of options.

Menu bars can also have toolbars below them, which can also be used to access related items. For example, in the **Paint** app there is a top Menu bar and a toolbar below it. Additional menus can be accessed from both of these.

Don't forget

The arrowhead next to an item on the toolbar indicates that there are additional options available to be displayed.

Some apps have commands that open dialog boxes that allow you to apply detailed configurations and settings. For instance, in the Notepad app, if **File** > **Page setup** is selected from the Menu bar, this opens a dialog box: the **OK** and **Cancel** buttons can be used to action or cancel the options selected in the dialog box.

Moving and Resizing Windows

1 To maximize a window, double-click the **Title bar** area (double-click again to restore the window to its original size)

2 To move a window, click the **Title bar** area, hold down the mouse button and drag the window

Double-clicking on the **Title bar** has the same effect as the **Maximize** and **Restore** buttons.

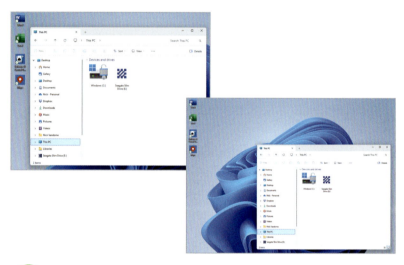

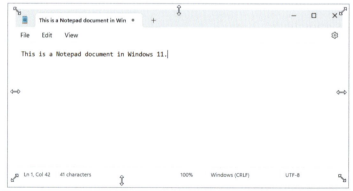

3 To resize a window, move the mouse pointer over any border or any corner

Dragging a corner of a window allows you to adjust two adjacent borders at the same time.

4 When the desired double-headed **Resize** arrow appears, click and drag until the frame displayed is the required size. Release the pointer, and the window is resized

4 Personalizing your System

Settings

Windows 11 provides the **Settings** function to make changes to your system. There are several ways to open **Settings**:

1 Click on the **Settings** app on the Taskbar

2 Press **WinKey** + **I** to open **Settings** directly

3 Press **WinKey** + **X**, or right-click on the **Start** button and select **Settings**

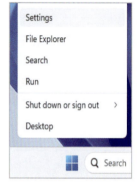

By default, the Settings app opens at the **Home** section, which displays general information about your Windows 11 computer and some recommended settings.

4 Click on the **Start** button and click on **All**. Select **Settings** from the alphabetic list

5 However the settings are accessed, the main categories appear in the left-hand sidebar. Click on a main category to view its content in the main **Settings** window

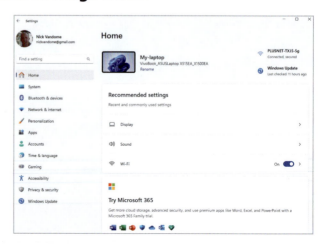

Settings categories

The categories of settings, accessed from the left-hand panel of the Settings app, are:

- **System**. These settings provide numerous options to specify how your computer looks and operates.

- **Bluetooth & devices**. These settings provide options for how the hardware connected with your computer operates.

- **Network & internet**. These settings provide options related to connecting to networks, usually for accessing the internet.

- **Personalization**. These settings provide options for customizing the look and feel of Windows 11.

- **Apps**. These settings provide options for specifying how apps work and interact with Windows 11.

- **Accounts**. These settings provide options for adding new online accounts (such as a new email account or an online storage and sharing service).

- **Time & language**. These settings provide options for the time zone used by your computer and the format for these items.

- **Gaming**. These settings contain a range of options for playing games on a Windows 11 computer.

- **Accessibility**. These settings are divided into three sections, for **Vision**, **Hearing**, and **Interaction**.

- **Privacy & security**. These settings can be used for a wide range of options for managing your data, and also security settings for keeping your computer as well protected as possible.

- **Windows Update**. These settings provide options for installing updates to Windows, and also backing up and recovering data on your computer.

Some of the settings have been updated in the Windows 11 2024 Update.

One very useful setting is for adding a printer to your computer. To do this, connect your printer to your computer and turn it on. Click on the **Bluetooth & devices** section, choose the **Printers & scanners** option, then click on the **Add device** button for **Add a printer or scanner**.

69

...cont'd

Working with settings

It is worth spending some time with the settings, as they can be invaluable in terms of managing Windows 11 and also customizing it so that you can create a look and feel with which you are most comfortable. To find your way around the settings:

1 Click on a category in the left-hand sidebar of the **Settings** app to view its details in the main window

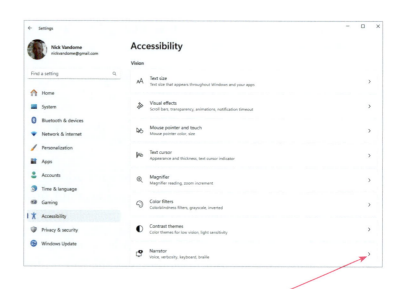

Hot tip

If the left-hand navigation panel in the **Settings** app is not visible (for instance, if the window has been reduced in size by resizing), click on this button on the top toolbar to view the navigation sidebar.

2 Click on a right-pointing arrow to access more options for a specific setting

3 Drag buttons **On** or **Off** to apply or disable specific settings

4 Click on the left-pointing arrow in the top left-hand corner of the **Settings** window to go back to the previous page being viewed in the **Settings** app

The feature is an easy way to change some of the settings on your PC. To display :

1 Click the Taskbar below the Wi-Fi icon and the Volume icon (or press the **WinKey + A** key combination)

The contents of depend on the particular system. This example shows the entries for a typical laptop.

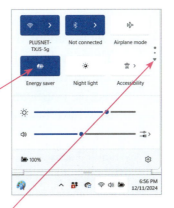

The interface of the panel has been updated in the Windows 11 2024 Update.

2 Click on the buttons to activate each item (the buttons are blue when they are active)

3 Click on these buttons to move between the sections

Drag these sliders in the panel to change the system brightness and volume levels.

4 Click on this button to access the full Settings section, or right-click on a button and click on **Go to Settings**

Keeping Focus

How you receive notifications can be personalized to ensure that you only get them when you want, using the **Focus** function. To do this:

The Focus function has been updated in the Windows 11 2024 Update.

1 Open the **Settings** app and click on the **Focus** option within the **System** section

2 Details about the potential focus session are displayed. These include showing and hiding certain functions and turning on **do not disturb** so that you do not receive notifications from any of your apps (unless they have been given permission; see the Hot tip)

Even if **do not disturb** is turned on, apps can still be given permission to use notifications. This can be done in **Settings > System > Notifications > Set priority notifications**.

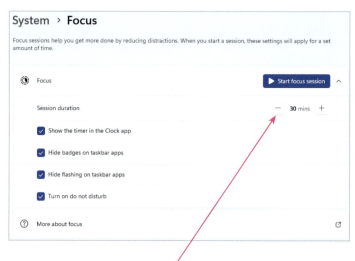

3 Click on the **-** and **+** buttons to set the duration for the focus session and click on the **Start focus session** button

4 Click on the **Stop focus session** button to stop the focus settings being applied

Personalizing the Lock Screen

The **Lock** screen appears when you start Windows 11, sign out, or resume from sleep. To customize this screen:

1 Open **Settings** then select the **Personalization** > **Lock screen** option

You can also open the **Personalization** settings by right-clicking the desktop and selecting the **Personalize** option.

2 Scroll down and select one of the supplied pictures as the image for your **Lock** screen

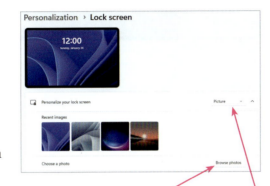

You can choose to display all the contents of your **Pictures** library in the form of a slideshow that runs on the **Lock** screen. This is accessed from the **Personalize your lock screen** option at the top of the window.

3 Alternatively, click **Browse photos** to select an image from your **Pictures** library or another image folder

4 Select the required picture and click **Choose picture**

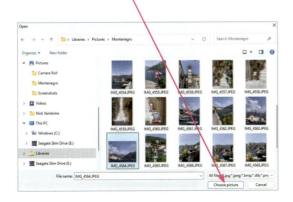

73

...cont'd

5 The selected item appears on the Lock screen, as indicated at the top of the **Personalization** > **Lock screen** window

Hot tip

Click in the **Lock screen status** box

and select an app, as required, to use on the Lock screen.

6 The picture you select can also appear on the **Sign in** screen, by dragging this button **On**

7 Check **On** the **Get fun facts, tips, tricks, and more on your lock screen** option to activate this feature

☑ Get fun facts, tips, tricks, and more on your lock screen

8 Any items that have been selected (in Step 7 above or in the tip) are displayed on the Lock screen

Desktop

1 Select **Settings** >
Personalization >
Background

2 Choose **Picture** from the drop-down menu and
select an image to act as the background for the
desktop

3 You can click **Browse photos** and select an image
from your Pictures library or another folder

4 Select
Personalization >
Start to control which
items are shown on the
Start menu

5 Select
Personalization
> **Colors** to apply
a color accent to the
Taskbar, window
borders and Start menu

6 Select **Fonts** to display the fonts available on your
system and get more fonts from the Microsoft Store

7 Select **Themes** to apply predefined sets of colors,
images and sound effects, and other related settings

If you signed in with
a Microsoft Account,
your choices will
be applied to any
Windows 11 PC you
sign in to with that
Microsoft Account.

Background can be
set as a
picture, a
slideshow,
or simply
a solid
color. The
image may
be made to
fill the screen;
fit to height;
stretch both
ways; tile;
center; or
span across
multiple monitors.

Account Picture

You can specify an image that will be displayed with your username wherever it appears.

1 Open **Settings** > **Accounts** > **Your info**

2 Click **Browse files** to select an existing image from your **Pictures** library or another image folder

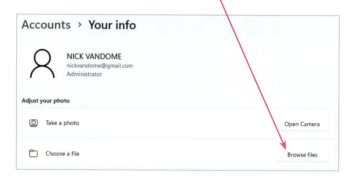

3 Select the required image and click on the **Choose picture** button

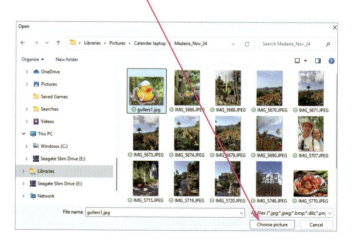

4 Alternatively, if your computer has a webcam or a built-in camera, select **Open Camera** in Step 2 to take a picture or a short video, of up to five seconds

Don't forget

Each username will have the default user image assigned, but this can be replaced by a more suitable image.

Don't forget

You can specify a picture of any size, but preferably a square image, and it will be reconstructed for use when signing in, etc.

76

Managing the Start Menu

The apps initially pinned to your Start menu depend on choices made by the manufacturer or supplier of your computer and will be in no particular sequence. However, you can add and remove apps to suit your requirements.

Turn on the **Show recently added apps** option, which will appear in the **Recommended** section.

You can also choose **Show most used apps**, at the top of the **All** list.

To customize the Start menu:

1 Select **Settings** > **Personalization** > **Start**

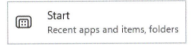

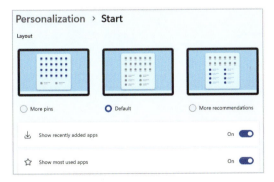

2 You can accept the **Default** option, choose **More pins** to see more apps, or select **More recommendations** (and therefore fewer pinned apps)

...cont'd

3 Select the **Folders** option within **Start**

📁 Folders
These folders appear on Start next to the Power button

4 Choose which of the system folders you'd like to appear on the Start menu

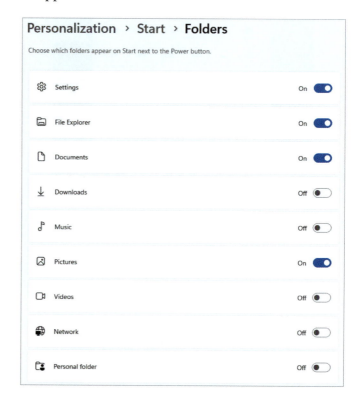

Personalization › Start › Folders

Choose which folders appear on Start next to the Power button.

⚙ Settings	On
🗂 File Explorer	On
🗋 Documents	On
↓ Downloads	Off
🎵 Music	Off
🖼 Pictures	On
▭ Videos	Off
🌐 Network	Off
📇 Personal folder	Off

Hot tip

You can right-click the row of icons on the Start menu and select **Personalize this list**, to redisplay the folders and revise your choice.

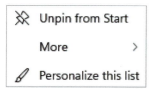

✂ Unpin from Start

More   ›

✎ Personalize this list

5 Click the **On/Off** button to display/hide the icon for each of the folders

The icons for the chosen folders are displayed at the foot of the Start menu, next to the **Power** button.

Nick Vandome   🗋 🖼 🗂 ⚙ ⏻

Managing Apps

Apps on the Start menu offer differing options, depending on the type of app and where it is located on the Start menu. Options can be viewed by right-clicking on apps.

1 For a pinned app, right-click on it to view its related menu, including the **Pin to taskbar** option

↖	Move to front
⚔	Unpin from Start
✧	Pin to taskbar
⚙	App settings
🗑	Uninstall

You can add your own folders to the Start menu. Right-click a folder in **File Explorer** (see Chapter 5) and select **Pin to Start**.

↪	Share
✧	Pin to Quick access
✧	Pin to Start

2 Depending on the type of app, the options on the menu may differ to some degree

↖	Move to front
⚔	Unpin from Start
▣	Run as administrator
▯	Open file location
⚔	Unpin from taskbar
🗑	Uninstall

3 For apps on the **All** list, right-click on one to view its related menu, including the option for **Pin to Start**

✧	Pin to Start
	More >
🗑	Uninstall

4 Click on the **More** option in Step 3 above to view additional menu options for the selected app

⚔	Unpin from taskbar
▣	Run as administrator
▯	Open file location
	Don't show in this list

Grouping Apps

Apps can be grouped together in folders, and also on the Start menu.

Grouping in folders

To create a folder containing specific apps:

1 Add shortcuts to the desktop, as shown on page 61

2 Right-click the desktop and select **New > Folder**

3 Give the folder a new name, as required

4 Drag and drop each of the app shortcuts in turn into the new folder, or drag around them to select them all and move them all together

5 You will now have a folder on the desktop that contains shortcuts for all of the apps on the desktop. Double-click on a shortcut to open an app

Hot tip

Double-click the folder icon to open it and reveal its contents.

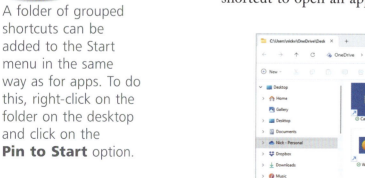

Hot tip

A folder of grouped shortcuts can be added to the Start menu in the same way as for apps. To do this, right-click on the folder on the desktop and click on the **Pin to Start** option.

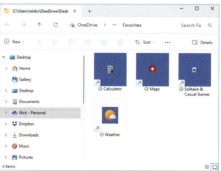

Grouping on the Start menu

Apps that have been pinned to the Start menu can also be grouped together into new folders. To do this:

1 Identify the apps to be grouped on the Start menu

Being able to group apps on the Start menu is a new feature in the Windows 11 2024 Update.

2 Drag one app over the other to create a folder

3 The two apps are displayed on the Start menu in the new folder, with a default name of **Folder**

4 Click on the folder to open it and view the contents. Click on **Edit name** to change the folder name

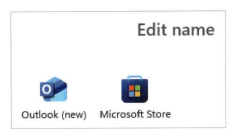

Beware

It is not possible to pin a folder on the Start menu to the Taskbar.

5 Enter a new folder name, as required

Hot tip

To remove an app from a folder, click and hold on it and drag it out of the folder, back onto the Start menu.

6 The new folder name appears on the Start menu

User Accounts

To allow several users to share the same PC, you give everyone their own sign-in (username and password) and access to their own files, browsers, and desktop settings.

Each user could have a Local account, just for that one PC, or a Microsoft Account that can be used on any PC on your network. The accounts you create will be of two types: **Standard** or **Administrator**.

Standard account

By default, when you create an account it will be a **Standard** account that can use most apps and change basic system settings that do not affect other users.

Administrator account

This is an elevated account that has complete access to the PC and can make account-type changes and modifications to the system that can impact all users.

User accounts can be specified when they are created, and they can also be changed at any time. To do this:

Beware

Only create an Administrator account for someone if you are happy for them to have the highest level of control over your computer.

1 Click on the **Accounts** tab in the **Settings** app

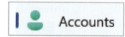

2 Click on the **Other users** option

3 Click on a user account and click on the **Change account type** button

4 Click here and select the account type, as required. Click on the **OK** button

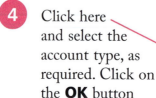

Changing the User Account

1 Select **Settings** > **Accounts** > **Your info**

2 If you signed in with a Microsoft Account, you can switch to a Local account by clicking on the **Sign in with a local account instead** option

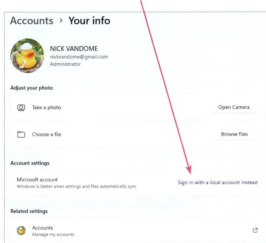

You'll be asked to provide an email address, which may be for an existing Microsoft Account or one that can be used to create such an account.

3 Click on the **Close and back up** button to back up the contents of your computer before you change to a Local account, or click on **Skip this step** to follow a step-by-step process for switching to a Local account

You must provide a username, password, and password hint to aid signing in to this computer. Note that as a Local account, it will not be synced with your other Windows computers. More options are available if you use your Microsoft Account.

New User Account

Family members can be added to your Windows 11 device so that they can use their own account with it. To do this:

Hot tip

You can add other users as part of your Family group, giving them an account of their own with libraries and standard folders.

1 Select **Settings > Accounts > Family**

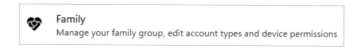

> ❤️ **Family**
> Manage your family group, edit account types and device permissions

2 Click on the **Add someone** button

> **Your family**
> Add someone to your family group and allow them to sign in on this device   [Add someone]

Don't forget

If the new user does not already have a Microsoft Account, you can create one as part of the process of adding the user's account.

3 Provide the email address for the person's Microsoft Account and click **Next**

Microsoft account   ✕

Add someone

Enter their email address

No Microsoft account? Create one for a child

[Cancel]   [Next]

Don't forget

The username is added to the list of users shown on the **Sign in** screen.

4 Select a role for the new person, and click **Invite** to offer the option to join your Family group

5 The new user receives an email with an invitation to join the Family group. The user should click **Accept Invitation** to join the group. No action needs to be taken if the decision is not to join

You can add non-family members to the **Other Users** section of **Accounts**.

1 Select **Settings > Accounts > Other Users > Add account**

2 Follow the prompts, providing the user's email details when requested, to add the new user

Hot tip

You may find on your system that you must select **Family & Other Users** to locate the **Other Users** option.

This user will be able to sign in to the PC, even if the existing account remains logged on to the computer.

1 From the Start menu, the new user should click the current user and select their name from the list

Don't forget

If you sign out, switch users or shut down and restart, the new user account can be selected from the **Sign in** screen.

2 On the **Sign in** screen that appears, type the password and press the **Enter** button

Windows creates user libraries and folders and installs any necessary apps. Progress messages are displayed. When setup completes, Windows returns with the new user account active and ready for use.

Setting up a Kiosk

With a PC set up as a **Kiosk**, you restrict the computer to a single app. This is an alternative to the **Guest** user, which was offered in some previous versions of Windows.

1 Select **Settings** > **Accounts** > **Other Users**) > **Kiosk**

2 Click **Get started** and enter a name for your Kiosk account, then click the **Next** button

3 Choose an app that is to be used on the Kiosk, then click **Next**. In this case, **Microsoft Edge** is selected

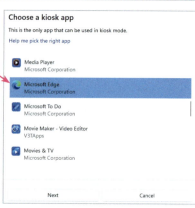

4 Select how the Kiosk is going to be used, and click the **Next** button

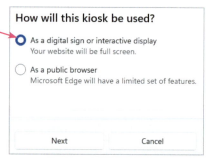

Don't forget

It isn't essential to restart your PC to apply the changes and make the newly defined account available for use.

5 Enter a website address for the homepage of the new Kiosk, when it opens, and click on the **Next** button

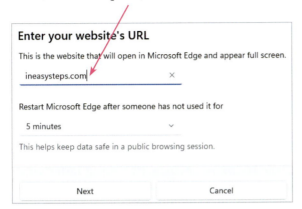

Any data that the app needs must be preloaded as it isn't possible to run any other apps while the assigned-access app is running, since there's no Taskbar, no Start menu, and no way to switch apps.

6 Click on the **Close** button to finish setting up the Kiosk

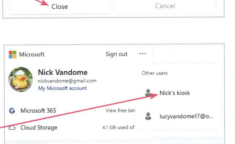

7 The new Kiosk is added to your accounts page. The Kiosk will open when the computer is restarted

To delete a Kiosk, access it in **Settings** > **Accounts** > **Other Users** > **Kiosk**. Click on the down-pointing arrowhead next to the Kiosk name and click on the **Remove kiosk** button.

To terminate the use of the Kiosk account, enter the **Ctrl + Alt + Del** key combination to return to the **Sign in** screen, where you can switch users.

To finish completely, left-click the **Power** symbol and select **Shut down**. Other options include **Sleep** and **Restart**. If there are updates pending, you may be offered **Update and shut down** or **Update and restart** options.

87

PIN codes are usually four digits and meant for tablet PCs, but can be used with any Windows 11 PC. You can use letters and symbols as well as digits (up to 127 characters in total).

You can return to **Sign-in options** at any time to change your PIN code, to remove the PIN as a sign-in option (if available), or to reset a forgotten PIN code.

PIN Code

1 Select **Settings > Accounts > Sign-in options** and choose **PIN (Windows Hello)**

2 Click **Next** to create a PIN (and enter your Microsoft password if prompted)

3 Enter four or more digits for the PIN and re-enter the numbers to confirm the PIN code

4 Select **OK** when the values have been entered

When you next sign in, you'll be asked for the PIN. You just provide the code itself – there's no need to press **Enter**.

The PIN codes that you define will apply only to the particular computer on which they have been specified and will not be transferred to any other computer on which you may choose to enable your Microsoft Account.

Display Settings

1 Right-click the desktop and select **Display settings** from the list

You can also open **Settings**, select **System**, and then choose **Display**.

2 Adjust the brightness of the display, in **Color profile**, turn on **Night light**, and enable **HDR** (high dynamic range) – if supported by your computer

3 Scroll down for more options

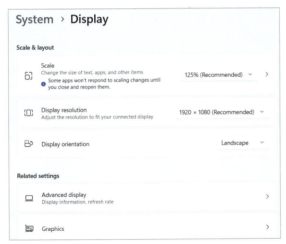

Screens emit blue light, which may be less comfortable at night, so you can turn on **Night light** in Step 1, and your monitor will display warmer colors.

4 A scaling factor for text and apps will be recommended, but you can change this to suit your preference

69

...cont'd

The resolutions and color settings offered depend on the type of monitor and the type of graphics adapter that you have on your computer.

The screen thumbnails will change to reflect resolution and orientation changes. You can also drag and drop the thumbnails to match the physical organization.

5 Click the **Display resolution** box to see the alternatives available

6 Choose a new resolution that you want to use, if the recommended option doesn't suit your requirements

| 1920 × 1080 (Recommended) |
| 1680 × 1050 |
| 1600 × 900 |
| 1440 × 900 |
| 1400 × 1050 |
| 1366 × 768 |

The higher the resolution, the more information you will fit on the screen but, of course, the text and images displayed will be smaller.

7 Click the **Display orientation** box to select **Landscape** or **Portrait**. Either can be flipped if required

| Landscape |
| Portrait |
| Landscape (flipped) |
| Portrait (flipped) |

Adjustments to **Color profile**, **Night light**, or **Scale** will be applied immediately, but when revisions of any other settings are applied, you will be asked to confirm that you want to keep the changes you have made.

1 If you want to retain the display settings as shown, click **Keep changes**

2 To undo the changes, select **Revert**, or simply wait 15 seconds and the changes will be reversed

Accessibility Settings

Making Windows 11 accessible for as wide a range of users as possible is an important consideration, and there are a range of accessibility settings that can be used for this. To configure these:

1 Open **Settings** and click on the **Accessibility** tab

2 Select options in the main panel. The main headings are for **Vision**, **Hearing**, and **Interaction**

3 Each option has settings that can be applied. For instance, drag the **Narrator** button from **Off** to **On** to enable items to be read out on the screen

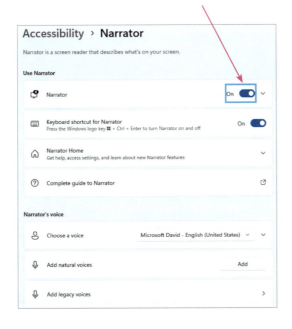

The settings for **Narrator** can be used to specify items on the screen that are read out. For some items, such as buttons and controls, there is an audio description of the item.

There is also a **Braille** option that can be accessed toward the bottom of the **Narrator** window. This has to be used in conjunction with third-party software that communicates with a Braille display.

...cont'd

4 Select **Magnifier** in Step 2 on page 91, and turn Magnifier **On** to activate the magnifying glass. Move this over areas to magnify them

To make the typing cursor easier to spot, select **Text cursor** in the **Vision** section and drag the **Size** slider to suit your needs.

You can also adjust the thickness value of the text cursor and choose a color that stands out in your text.

5 Select the **Contrast themes** option in Step 2 on page 91, and click in the **Contrast themes** box to select a color theme for text and background for users who find it difficult reading black text on a white background

6 In the **Hearing** section, click on the **Captions** option then drag the **Live captions** button **On** to enable captions for compatible audio and video content

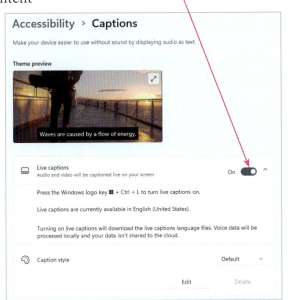

7 In the **Interaction** section, select **Mouse** to choose to use the numeric keypad to move the mouse, and adjust the color, size, and speed of the mouse pointer. Drag the **Mouse keys** button **On** to access the available options

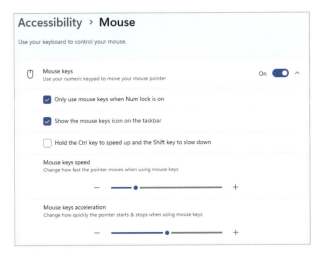

The **Vision** settings are Text size, Visual effects, Mouse pointer and touch, Text cursor, Magnifier, Color filters, Contrast themes, and Narrator. The **Hearing** settings are Audio, Hearing devices and Captions. The **Interaction** settings are Speech, Keyboard, Mouse, and Eye control.

Opening the Control Panel

In previous versions of Windows, the most comprehensive options for customizing your system were provided via the **Control Panel**. Although the **Settings** feature is now taking over, the **Control Panel** can still be used for some functions, although it is more hidden away these days. To access the **Control Panel**:

Another way to access the **Control Panel** is to select **Windows Tools** from the **All** list and click on the **Control Panel** option.

1 Click on the **Search** icon on the Taskbar

2 Enter "control panel" in the Search box. When the **Control Panel** entry appears, click it or press **Enter**

3 Options for the **Control Panel** are displayed

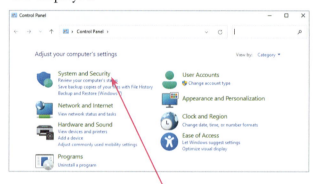

Don't forget

Click on the **Category** button in the top right of the **Control Panel** window to select options for how items in the **Control Panel** are displayed.

4 Click on one of the main categories to view its contents

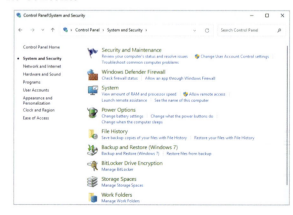

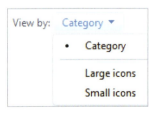

94

5 The Power of the Internet

Windows 11 uses the Microsoft Edge internet browser to help you navigate through the web. This chapter shows how to get started with some of its functions and features, including making a quick connection.

In order to access the internet, by any method, you need to sign up with an Internet Service Provider (ISP). They will provide the necessary Wi-Fi connection and usually provide the router for physically connecting to Wi-Fi, too.

Your system may detect other wireless networks that are in the vicinity, so make sure to select the correct entry.

Quick Internet Connections

Being able to quickly connect to the internet is now an essential part of everyday computing. With Windows 11, this can be done within the **Network & internet** section of the Settings app. There is also an option within the Quick Settings panel so that an internet connection is only a click away. To do this with Quick Settings:

1 Move the mouse cursor over the **Network** icon on the right of the Taskbar

2 This shows **No internet access**, **Connections available**

3 Click on this button to display the available Wi-Fi networks

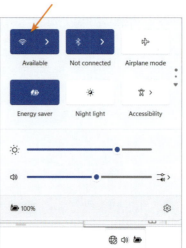

4 Click on the required wireless network

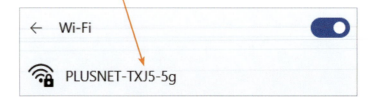

5 Check the **Connect automatically** box **On** and then click on the **Connect** button

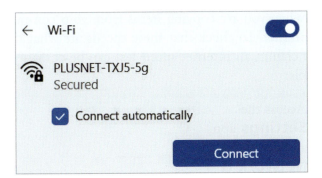

6 Enter the password for the router to be used to connect to the Wi-Fi network and click on the **Next** button

7 The Wi-Fi connection is displayed with the words **Connected, secured** below it

If the **Connect automatically** option is checked **On** in Step 5, your computer will now always connect to that network when it comes into range.

97

Internet Speed Test

When you sign up with an Internet Service Provider they should give you speeds for downloading data from the internet – e.g. for movies and music, and for uploading data, such as when you are copying items from your computer to the internet. To check that these speeds are what the provider claims, an internet speed test can be performed. To do this:

1 Access the **Settings** app and select **Network & internet > Wi-Fi**

2 Click on the **Run an internet speed test** option under the **Related support** heading

3 The Edge web browser opens, displaying options for conducting an internet speed test. Scroll down the page to view different options, or click on the **Start** button

Don't forget

Internet download and upload speeds are measured in megabytes per second (Mb/s).

4 The internet speed test starts by checking the download speed

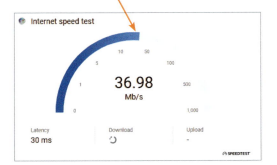

5 When the download speed test is completed the result is displayed, and the test for the upload speed starts automatically

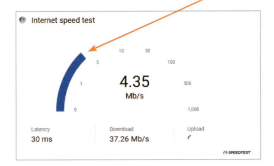

6 When the speed test is completed the results for download and upload speeds are displayed. Click on the **Rerun** button to perform the speed test again

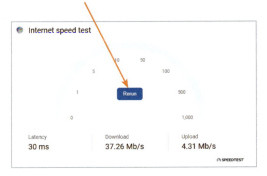

Don't forget

Another item that is displayed during the speed test is latency. This refers to the speed at which your computer and the internet respond to commands that have been made, such as clicking on a link on a web page. It is measured in milliseconds (ms).

Browsing the Web

By default, Windows 11 provides access to the internet via the Microsoft Edge browser.

1 Click the **Microsoft Edge** icon on the Taskbar, or from the Start menu, to open the app

Don't forget

See pages 215-216 for details about connecting to a network for access to the internet.

2 The screen displays the **Start** page, with a search box and recommended websites

3 Click on the **Settings** icon to display page settings

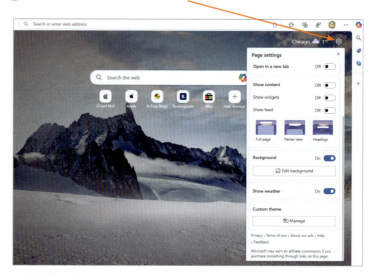

You can scroll the screen with the mouse wheel, or by clicking the scroll bar that appears when you move the mouse, or by dragging the scroll bar on a touch monitor.

4 Click in the **Search** box at the top of the Start page and begin typing your search term – "ineasy", for example – to see related search suggestions

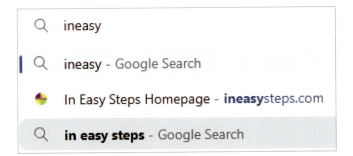

Favorites gives access to the **Favorites bar**.

5 Choose a search suggestion to see a list of web pages matching that term

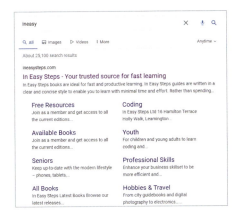

Settings and more (**...**) gives access to a variety of options.

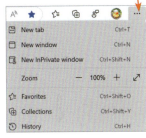

6 Select one of the web pages and explore the commands that are available

Back/Forward   Address bar   Collections

Refresh   New tab   Read aloud   Favorites

Favorites

You can make your more frequently accessed web pages easier to find using **Favorites**. To do this, first open the web page that you want to make a favorite.

1. Click on the star icon at the right-hand side of the Address bar

2. Name your chosen web page, specify the folder – in this case, the **Favorites bar** – and click **Done** to complete

3. The chosen web page is added to the list of favorites, indicated by the star icon being filled with a solid color

4. Click the **Add folder** button to create a new folder on the **Favorites bar**, and specify a folder name

5. Click the **Favorites** icon on the Microsoft Edge Toolbar, and the favorites will be displayed

...cont'd

By default, Microsoft Edge will show the **Favorites bar** only on a new tab, but you can display it in other situations.

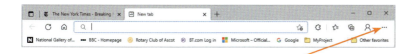

1 Select **Settings and more (...)** > **Settings**

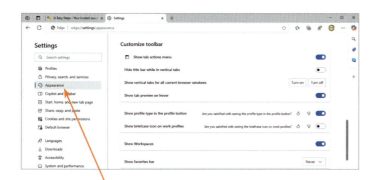

Hot tip

You can also show and hide the sidebar, at the right-hand side of the Edge window, that gives access to other apps, by selecting **Settings and more (...)** > **Settings** > **Copilot and sidebar**, and choosing **Always on**, **Auto hidden** or **Off**.

2 Select **Appearance** and scroll to **Customize toolbar**

3 Click the **Down** arrow and choose the **Always** option for **Show favorites bar**

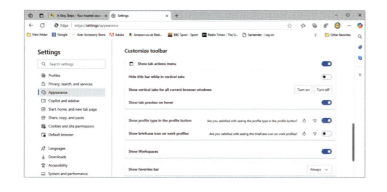

4 Microsoft Edge will now feature the **Favorites bar**, which appears just below the **Address bar**

Viewing site information has been updated in the Windows 11 2024 Update.

Ensure that **Tracking prevention for this side (Balanced)** in Step 2 is turned **On**, to prevent websites following your activity on the web. Click on the **Trackers** option to view details for blocked items.

Click on this icon in the **Address bar**, if available, to enable the Edge browser to read aloud the content on the current page being viewed (see page 101):

Viewing Site Information

From a security and privacy point of view, it is important to be able to view information about the websites that you visit, to ensure that your browsing experience is as safe as possible. To do this with the Edge browser:

1 Access the required web page and click on this icon at the left-hand side of the Address bar

2 The site information details and options are displayed

3 Click on the **Connection is secure** option in Step 2 to view details about the internet connection, including whether the site has a security certificate

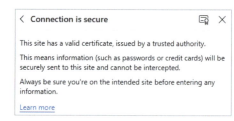

4 Click on the **Cookies and site data** option in Step 2 to view details about cookies (small programs that collect browsing data on websites) that are being used on the page and how to manage them

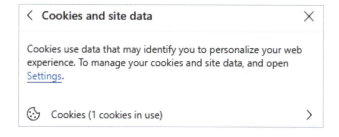

Settings

There is an extensive range of settings that can be used with the Edge browser.

1 Select **Settings and more (...)** and click on the **Settings** button

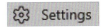

2 The main settings categories are listed in the left-hand sidebar. Click on a category to view its content in the main window

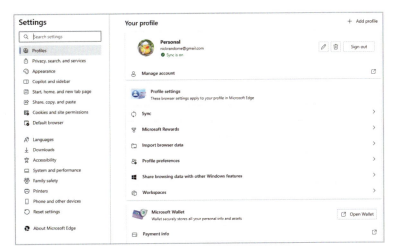

3 Select the **Privacy, search, and services** category to apply a range of security settings

4 Select the **Appearance** category to apply options for how Edge windows look

5 Select the **Start, home, and new tab page** category to apply settings for how certain items open up in the Edge browser

Don't forget

You can clear browsing data that may build up on your system by selecting **Choose what to clear** in the **Privacy, search, and services** category (further down the screen in Step 3).

Light and Dark Themes

Microsoft Edge offers a choice of display themes.

1 Open a web page, and the **System default** theme will be applied to all displayed Microsoft Edge menus; for example, **History**

2 From **Settings and more (...)** > **Settings**, select **Appearance** in the left-hand sidebar

3 The Edge themes are displayed. Choose a theme – e.g. the **Dark** option

4 The selected theme is immediately applied to all related items

5 The content of the web page itself is unchanged

Hot tip

Experiment with the Light and Dark themes at different times of day, and in different lighting conditions, to find the best combination.

Screen Capture

With Microsoft Edge, you can save parts of web pages; useful when you wish to share information with others.

1 Open a web page that you want to save and click **Settings and more** (...) > **Settings**

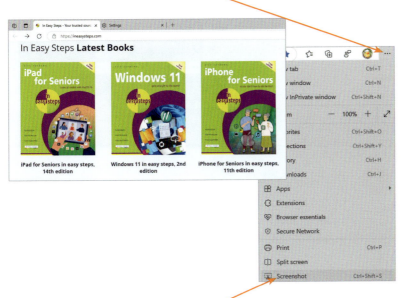

2 Click the **Screenshot** option and choose an option – **Capture area, Capture screen area** or **Capture full page**

3 Drag over the screen to capture a specific area

Hot tip

When you have selected an area or a full page, you can mark up the selection and copy it to a file.

Right-click Menus

Additional functionality can be viewed on web pages with the Microsoft Edge browser, by using the right-click option on the mouse. To do this:

Hot tip

You can view multiple pages in Microsoft Edge, each on a separate tab (see pages 109-111).

1 Open a web page in Microsoft Edge

2 Right-click an empty part of the page (the mouse pointer remains as an arrow) to get a basic context menu

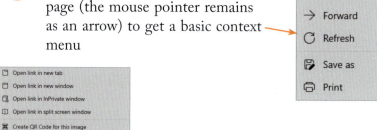

Don't forget

Hyperlinks direct you to other website locations. They can be associated with images, graphics, and text.

3 Right-click an image with a hyperlink (the mouse pointer becomes a hand), and an image-related context menu appears

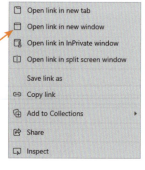

4 There is a more restricted context menu displayed when you right-click text with a hyperlink (again, with a hand pointer)

Tabbed Browsing

Being able to open several web pages at the same time in different tabs is a standard feature in most web browsers. To do this with Microsoft Edge:

1 Click on this button at the top of the Microsoft Edge window

2 Pages can be opened in new tabs using the smart **Address bar** or from any of the content options that are displayed on the page (which varies by location)

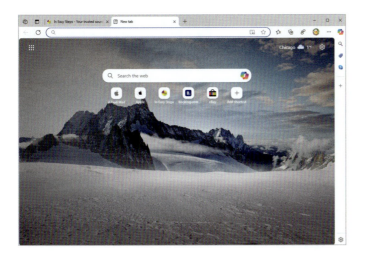

Hot tip

The **Start** page for new tabs, as displayed in Step 2, can be changed if required. To do this, open the Microsoft Edge settings and access the **Start, home, and new tabs** section. Check **On** the **Open the new tab page** option, then below the **When Edge starts** heading, select the **Add a new page** button.

109

Hot tip

Press **Ctrl** + **T** to add a new tab.

3 All open tabs are displayed at the top of the window. Click and hold on a tab to drag it into a new position

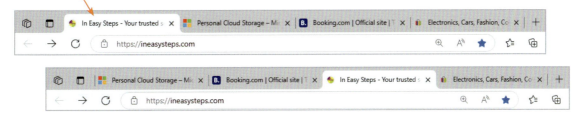

...cont'd

Once tabs have been opened in the Edge browser, there are a number of options for viewing and managing them.

1. Right-click on a tab to view options for managing tabs, including creating a new tab, duplicating the currently active tab, pinning tabs, and changing the orientation of open tabs

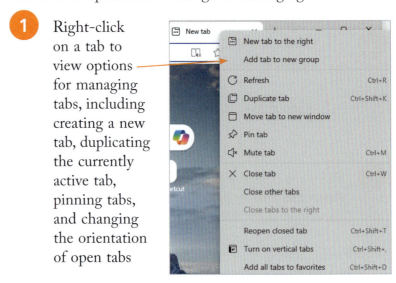

2. Click on this button at the left-hand side of the **Tabs bar** to access more options

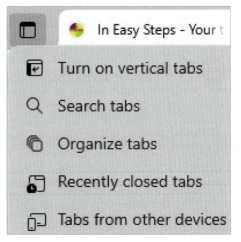

3. Click on the **Turn on vertical tabs** option to change the orientation of the **Tabs bar**

4 The **Tabs bar** is displayed down the left-hand side of the Edge browser window

5 Click on this button to maximize and minimize the vertical **Tabs bar**

111

6 Move the cursor over the minimized **Tabs bar** and click on this button to expand it, then click on the pin icon to keep the maximized option in place

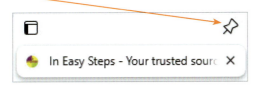

Zooming in on a Web Page

You may find some web pages difficult to read, especially if you have your monitor set for high resolution (see page 42). Microsoft Edge also provides a **Zoom** feature. Its methods for zooming the web page include:

Press **F11** on the keyboard to exit full-screen mode.

1 Select **Settings and more (...)**, and on the **Zoom** entry click the **+** or **-** buttons to zoom in, by 10% initially and then in increments of 25%, or zoom out

2 Click on this button to view the Edge window in full-screen mode

3 Press **Ctrl +** to zoom in, by 10% initially and then in increments of 25%, or **Ctrl -** to zoom out

4 Press **Ctrl 0** to reset to 100%

5 If the option with the **Ctrl** key is used, a magnifying glass icon appears in the **Address bar**. Click on the zoom options as required

6 Click on the **Reset** button to return to 100% view

6 Organizing

Windows 11 helps organize the files and folders on your hard disk, and also with the online storage and backup function, OneDrive. Content is stored in separate folders for different types of files, or you can add new folders. Libraries allow you to work with groups of folders. Powerful search options help you find your way around your folders.

File Explorer

Although **File Explorer** is not necessarily one of the first apps that you will use with Windows 11, it still plays an important role in organizing your folders and files. To access **File Explorer**:

1 From the desktop, click on this icon on the Taskbar, or

2 Press **WinKey** + **E**, and **File Explorer** opens at the **Home** folder

Hot tip

You can click on the **Start** button and access **File Explorer** from here too.

114

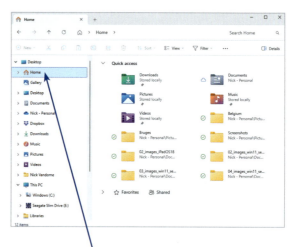

3 The locations on the computer are shown in the left-hand navigation pane

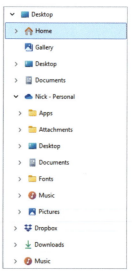

...cont'd

File Explorer Menu bar

The **Menu bar** in **File Explorer** has been simplified in Windows 11, replacing the **Scenic Ribbon**, but it can still be used for a variety of tasks for viewing and managing items within **File Explorer**.

1 The **Menu bar** is displayed at the top of **File Explorer**, regardless of which window is being viewed. If nothing is selected in **File Explorer**, a number of options are unavailable (grayed out)

2 Click on an item within a **File Explorer** window to activate more of the options on the **Menu bar**

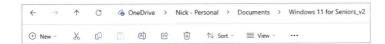

3 Click on the down-pointing arrow next to an item in the **Menu bar** to access its additional options for the current **File Explorer** window

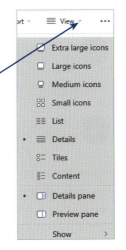

4 Click on this button (**See more**) to view more options for a selected item

Right-click anywhere within a **File Explorer** window to access the **File Explorer** context menu; i.e. one that applies to the item in the current window.

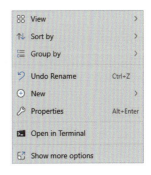

115

Files and Folders

The hardware components are the building blocks for your computer, but it is the information on your hard disk that really makes your computer operate. There is a huge number of files and folders stored there, in **File Explorer**. To get an idea of how many:

1 Double-click on **This PC** in the left-hand navigation pane

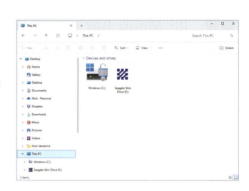

2 When **File Explorer** opens, double-click the **OS (C:)** drive to reveal its contents

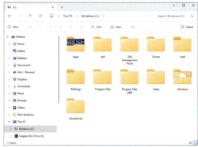

3 Press **Ctrl** + **A** to select all items in the specified drive

4 Right-click the selection and click **Properties**

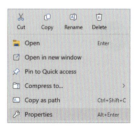

Hot tip

Select **View** > **Show** > **Hidden items** to obtain the full counts of files and folders.

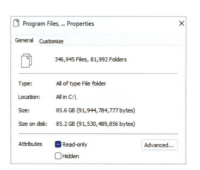

5 In this example, you see quoted counts of nearly 347,000 files and almost 82,000 folders on the **C:** drive, not including any hidden items (see the tip)

User Folders

Documents and pictures that you create or save on your computer are kept in folders associated with your username.

1 Open the **C:** drive in **File Explorer** (see the previous page), then select and double-click the **Users** folder

2 You will see a sub-folder for each user account name, plus the **Public** sub-folder

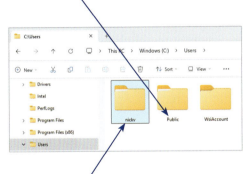

3 Double-click the folder for the active user – in this example, nickv

There is a set of sub-folders with all documents, pictures, data files, and settings belonging to that user. There's also a link to **OneDrive**, the online storage for that user.

Each user folder (including the **Public** folder) has a similar set of sub-folders defined.

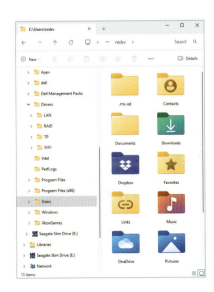

The **Public** folder is available to all user accounts and can be used to share files with other people using the same computer or those using other computers on the same network.

Don't forget

OneDrive has a **Personal Vault** folder that has added levels of security for storing your most sensitive and important documents and photos. It requires an extra level of security to access the Personal Vault; e.g. a PIN code or a code that is sent to you via email or text message. The Personal Vault can be accessed from any of the OneDrive interfaces.

Hot tip

Your OneDrive folder can be pinned to the Quick access section in File Explorer. To do this, right-click on the OneDrive icon in File Explorer and click on **Pin to Quick access**.

Using OneDrive

Cloud computing is now a mainstream part of our online experience. This involves saving content to an online computer (server) connected to the service that you are using – i.e. through your Microsoft Account. You can then access this content from any computer or mobile device using your account login details, and also share it with other people. It can also be used to back up your files in case they get corrupted or damaged on your computer.

The cloud service with Windows 11 is known as OneDrive, and you can use it with a Microsoft Account. It consists of the OneDrive folder in File Explorer, the OneDrive app, and the online OneDrive website. To get started with this:

1 On your computer, click on the **OneDrive** option on the **Start** menu. If this is the first time you have accessed OneDrive, click on the **Create account** button and follow the step-by-step process to link your Microsoft Account to OneDrive

2 Click on the **[Your name] - Personal** folder in File Explorer to view its contents

3 The contents of your OneDrive folder are displayed in File Explorer

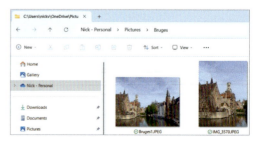

OneDrive App

The OneDrive app can be used on a Windows 11 computer, once it has been downloaded from the Microsoft Store. However, since OneDrive can be accessed directly through File Explorer, the need to use the app on a computer is reduced. Where it really comes into its own is when it is downloaded and used on a mobile device – such as a smartphone – so that you can always access the content in your OneDrive, wherever you are. To do this:

1. Access and download the OneDrive app from the app store linked to your mobile device – e.g. the Apple App Store or the Google Play Store

2. The OneDrive app will display all of the content from your Windows 11 computer that has been synced with OneDrive

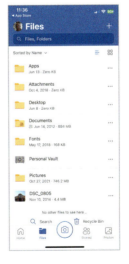

3. Click on the **+** button to add more content to the app, which will be available in OneDrive on your Windows 11 computer

119

Hot tip

By default, you get 5GB of free OneDrive storage space with Windows 11.
This is an excellent way to back up your important documents, since they are stored away from your computer.

Hot tip

In addition to using the OneDrive function to back up the content on your computer, this can also be done with an external hard drive or a memory stick. To do this, copy the items in File Explorer, select the required external hard drive or memory stick, and paste the items.

OneDrive Online

As with the OneDrive app, the online version of OneDrive can be used to access its contents when you are away from your Windows 11 computer. To view the contents of OneDrive online, go to the website at **microsoft.com/en-us/microsoft-365/onedrive/online-cloud-storage** and sign in with your Microsoft Account details.

Don't forget

If items are added to one version of OneDrive – e.g. the OneDrive app – they will also be available in the other versions too – e.g. the online version.

1 Your OneDrive content is the same as in your OneDrive folder on your computer, and in the OneDrive app

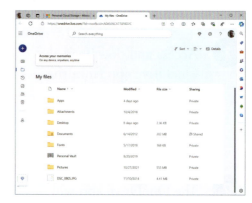

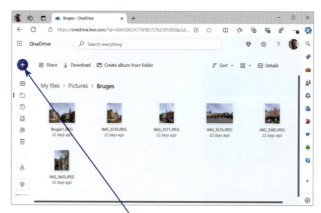

Hot tip

Click on individual files in OneDrive folders to select them. Once selected, a toolbar of options appears above the selected item(s).

2 Click on the **+** button to add more content to OneDrive online, which will be available in the OneDrive folder on your Windows 11 computer

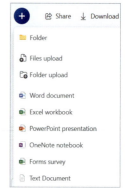

OneDrive Settings

The functionality of OneDrive becomes more integrated with Windows with each new version of the operating system. This is to ensure that you can back up as much of your important content as possible, without having to worry about it once it has been initially set up. This can be done with the OneDrive settings:

1 Right-click on the OneDrive icon in the Notifications area of the Taskbar

2 Click on the **Settings** option

3 In the **OneDrive Settings** window, click on the **Account** option in the left-hand sidebar

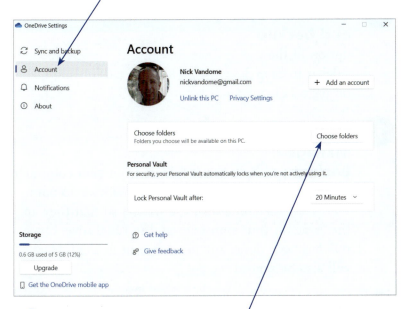

4 Click on the **Choose folders** button to select which OneDrive folders, and their content, will be displayed within File Explorer

Beware

The OneDrive icon in Step 1 is different from the OneDrive app icon that appears on the Start menu and that can be pinned to the main area of the Taskbar. The icon in Step 1 is only available in the Notifications area.

121

Don't forget

The Account section can also be used to unlink your PC so that files on your computer are not synced with the online OneDrive. Click on the **Unlink this PC** option to do this.

...cont'd

Don't forget

If the options are checked **Off** in Step 5, this only hides the folders from being displayed in File Explorer; it does not affect them being backed up by OneDrive, if this has been selected in Step 8.

5 Check the required folders **On** or **Off**, as required, to display them in File Explorer, or check **On** the **Make all files available** checkbox

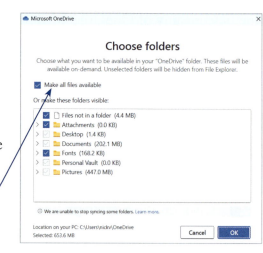

6 Click on the **Sync and backup** option in the sidebar in Step 3 on page 121

7 Click on the **Manage backup** option to select folders from your computer that you want to sync with your OneDrive account – i.e. copy the content of the folders so that they are the same on your computer and in OneDrive. Once this has been done, any new content in the folders will also be synced

8 Drag the buttons **On** or **Off** for the required items, and click on the **Close** button

OneDrive in File Explorer

Once OneDrive has been set up, and the required settings have been applied as on the previous page, this can affect how folders appear in File Explorer.

1 If folders have been turned **On** for **Sync and backup** as in Step 8 on the previous page, then they will be displayed with the OneDrive path at the top of File Explorer, regardless of how the folder is accessed in File Explorer

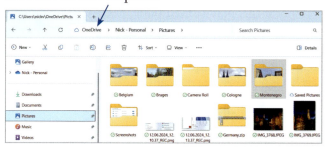

2 If a folder is turned **Off** in Step 8 on the previous page, the OneDrive path is not available and only the local folder – the one on your device – will be displayed

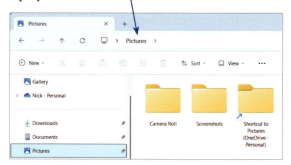

3 The full content of OneDrive can be viewed within File Explorer by clicking on the **[Your name] - Personal** option in the File Explorer sidebar

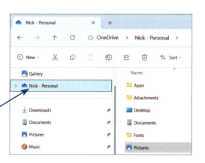

Hot tip

Content can be added to the OneDrive folder in File Explorer by saving it there when a document is first saved, copying it there using copy and paste, or dragging it there from another location in File Explorer.

Libraries

Libraries contain shortcuts to individual folders but allow you to treat the contents as if they were all in one folder. Typically, the **Documents** library would be a combination of the user's **Documents** folder and the **Public Documents** folder. This allows you to share documents with others (or access their documents). In Windows 11, libraries are not displayed by default, but you can add them to **File Explorer**.

1 Open **File Explorer** and right-click the Navigation pane, then select the **Show libraries** option

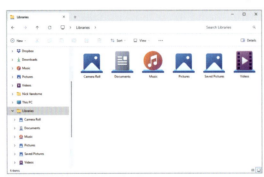

The Library folders do not have to be used, but it is a good way to see the actual physical location of your folders and files.

2 Select the **Libraries** entry that gets added, and you will see the expected four libraries – **Documents**, **Pictures**, **Music**, and **Videos**, plus (perhaps) **Saved Pictures** and **Camera Roll**, used by the **Photos** and **Camera** apps

3 Double-click on a folder – e.g. the **Pictures** library – and you will see it has files from two locations: the user's OneDrive **Pictures** folder (local copy of online folder) and the user's local **Pictures** folder

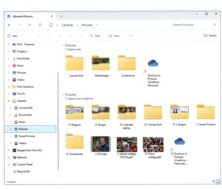

Folder Navigation

When you open a drive or folder, you will find a number of different ways to navigate around the folders on your disk.

1 Open, for example, a sub-folder in **Pictures** using **File Explorer**

Command bar   Menu bar   See more   Search box

Forward, Back

Up one level

Address bar

Navigation pane

Contents pane

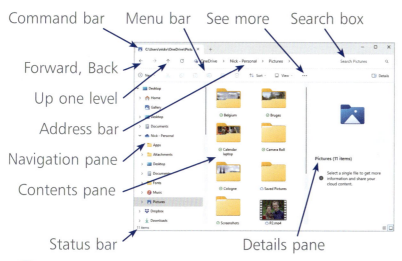

Status bar   Details pane

2 To go directly to a location on the **Address bar**, just click that location; for example, the user's folder

3 To go to a sub-folder of a location on the **Address bar**, click the arrow to the right of that location and select a sub-folder from the list displayed

4 To type a location, click at the right of the **Address bar**

5 The full address for the current location is shown highlighted

`C:\Users\nickv\OneDrive\Pictures\Saved Pictures`

6 Press **Enter** to go to that location

Click the **Forward** and **Back** arrows to navigate through locations you have already visited.

The **Address bar** displays the current location as a series of links, separated by arrows. There's an **Up** arrow at the left, to go up one level.

For common locations, you can type just the name; for example:
- Computer
- Contacts
- Control Panel
- Documents
- Pictures

125

Creating Folders and Files

1 Open the library or folder where the new folder is required; e.g. select **Documents**

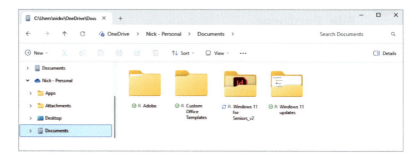

Create new folders to organize your documents by use or purpose, or create files of particular types, ready for use.

2 Right-click an empty part of the folder area and select **New > Folder**. Alternatively, you can select a specific file type

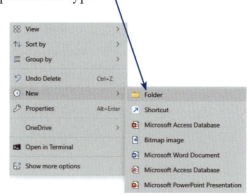

3 Overtype the name **New folder** with the required name, and press **Enter** (or click elsewhere)

If you create a folder or a file in a library, such as **Documents** or **Pictures**, it will be created and stored within the library's default save location; for example, the current user's **My Documents** or **My Pictures** folder.

Copying or Moving Files

You can copy one or more files using the Windows clipboard.

1 Open the folder containing the file, click the file icon to select it, and press **Ctrl + C**

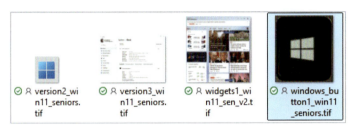

2 To copy multiple files, press the **Shift** or **Ctrl** keyboard keys and select all the files before pressing **Ctrl + C**

3 Locate and open the destination folder, right-click an empty space and press **Ctrl + V** to create a copy of the file(s) in that folder

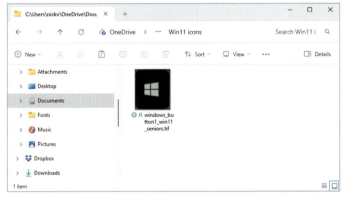

4 To move a file to a new location rather than make a copy, right-click the file icon and press **Ctrl + X**

5 The original file icon will be grayed out until you press **Ctrl + V** at the new location, and it will be moved there

You can right-click the file icon and select **Show more options** > **Copy**, to copy a file to the clipboard.

Also, right-click a folder and select **Show more options** > **Paste**, to copy a file from the clipboard.

Alternatively, right-click a file icon and select **Show more options** > **Cut** to initiate moving a file.

127

...cont'd

Hot tip

If the target folder isn't visible, locate it using the Navigation pane, clicking the gray arrows to expand the folders.

To move or copy files using drag and drop operations:

1 Use **File Explorer** to locate and open the folder containing files you want to move. Select one or more files, as required

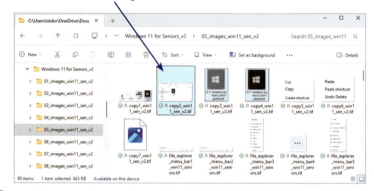

2 Drag the selection to the target folder, which should display the **Move** tag, and release there

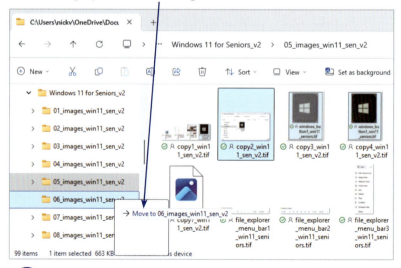

Don't forget

If you drag using the right mouse button rather than the left, when you release the files, you get a menu to confirm the desired action (or to cancel).

Copy here
Create shortcuts here
Cancel

Beware

When the source and target folders are on different drives, the **Shift** key activates **Copy**, and the **Ctrl** key activates **Move**.

3 To copy rather than move the selected files, hold down **Ctrl** as you drag and release the selection

+ Copy to Minutes

4 If the target folder is in a different drive, hold down **Shift** as you drag to move – otherwise, you will copy

Deleting Files

To remove files from a folder:

1 Select a file or files, and either right-click the selection and choose the **Delete** command or press the keyboard **Delete** key

2 If the file is located anywhere other than your hard disk, you are asked to confirm permanent deletion

3 Files on the hard disk are moved to the **Recycle Bin**, usually with the warning message turned off

To recover a file deleted by mistake:

1 Right-click the **Recycle Bin** icon and select **Open** (or just double-click the icon)

2 Select a file or files you want to recover

3 Click on **Restore the selected items** to return the file to its original location

The Recycle Bin is a folder that is pre-installed with Windows 11. It is where deleted items are placed so that they are not permanently deleted. It can be accessed from this icon on the desktop or from within File Explorer:

Before you permanently delete a file from your computer, copy it to an external hard drive or a flashdrive (USB stick), just in case you ever need it again.

Folder Views

File Explorer offers a variety of ways to view file and sub-folder entries that are contained in your folders and libraries. For example:

1 Open a library or folder, such as **Pictures**, and note the file list style used (in this case, **Large icons**)

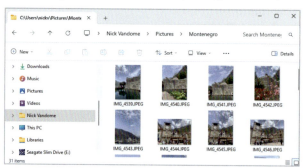

2 Right-click an empty part of the folder area and select **View** to see the various styles, with the current setting identified by a bullet point

3 Choose any of the four icon sizes offered to see how the folder contents are displayed

Extra large icons

Large icons

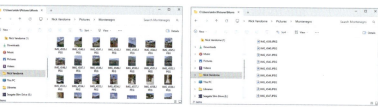

Medium icons   Small icons

From the **View** options you can choose **Show** > **Compact view** to decrease space between items and get to see more of the entries at once.

Other views can offer extra information about files.

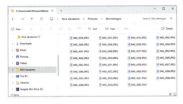

List

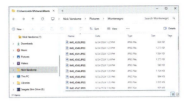

Details

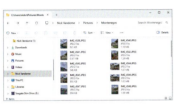

Tiles

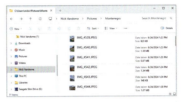

Content

A file-type icon rather than a thumbnail is used for **Small icons**, **List**, and **Details** views.

The details provided with the **Content** view depend on the file type and on the data provided when the file was created.

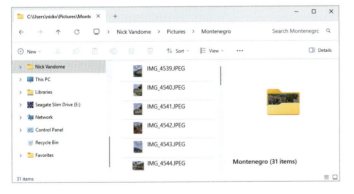

The options in the **Sort** menu also depend on the type of file for which the folder has been optimized. To illustrate:

Documents

Music

Videos

Downloads

The options in the sub-menus (**More** and **Group by**) will also be determined by the folder type.

Home Folder

To help you search for apps and to quickly access the ones you use frequently, Windows 11 has a directory within **File Explorer** called **Home**. This displays the **Quick access** and **Favorites** sections, where various files and folders can be added. To use the **Home** folder:

1. Open **File Explorer** and by default it will display the **Home** folder, consisting of **Quick access**, **Favorites**, and **Shared**

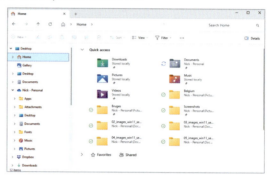

Hot tip

To change the default location that is displayed when File Explorer is opened, select the **See more (...)** option on the Menu bar and select **Options**. Click on the **General** tab and click in the **Open File Explorer to:** box, as shown on the next page.

2. Select **View > Show** and click the **Navigation pane** option to turn it **Off**

3. The **Home** folders are now displayed with the Navigation pane hidden

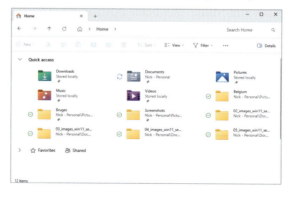

To add items to the **Home** folder:

1 Right-click a folder and select **Pin to Quick access**. The folder you select will appear in the **Quick access** section of the **Home** folder

2 Similarly, right-click a file and choose **Add to Favorites**, and it is added to the **Pinned files** section

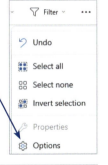

To show or hide the **Recents** section in the **Home** folder:

1 In **File Explorer**, click **See more (...)** and select **Options** to display the **Folder Options** panel

2 Select the **General** tab and choose **Open File Explorer to: > Home**

3 Click the **Show recently used files** and **Show frequently used folders** options (which puts checkmarks in the boxes), then click **OK**

Don't forget

To remove folders and files from the Home folder: for **Quick access** folders, right-click on a folder and select **Unpin from Quick access**; for **Favorites** files, right-click on the file and select **Unpin from Favorites**.

133

Don't forget

If you wish to avoid leaving records of your file and folder accesses, set **Privacy** options as unchecked, and click the **Clear** button to clear **File Explorer** history.

File Explorer Search Box

If you want to access a file but are not sure which sub-folder it is in, you can start at the higher-level folder and use the **Search** box to find the exact location.

1 Open **File Explorer** at any folder

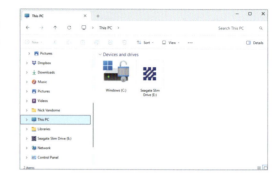

2 Click in the **Search** box and start typing the search words – for example: "windows"

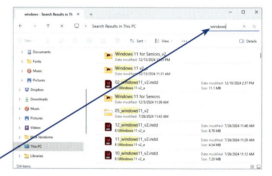

3 Add to the search criteria, as required. As you type, matching items will be listed

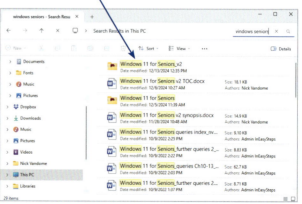

4 Stop typing when the results show the file you are seeking, or complete your search request to get the most compact list of references

7 Getting Things Done

Your Windows 11 computer can be used for practical options, such as online shopping, auctions and composing letters.

Shopping Online Securely

Online shopping is one of the great inventions on the internet, and it is easy to see why:

- A huge range of options, much larger than you would find in high street stores. This makes it easier to find even the most unusual items, and the online shopping environment is a global one, too.

- Competitive prices. Since online shops do not have the traditional costs of bricks and mortar stores, they can generally offer lower prices.

- Home delivery. This is a great convenience for online shopping, and it is a service that is generally getting quicker and quicker, with some online shopping sites now offering same-day delivery, if the items are ordered before a certain time. Look out for sites that offer free delivery, as this can make an online transaction even more cost-effective.

However, as with any websites that include financial transactions, it is important to ensure that the online shopping experience is as secure as possible, and the only thing that you have to worry about is which item to buy. Generally, the most reputable online shopping sites include a range of security features, to give users as much confidence as possible during the whole experience. Two of the main security features can be viewed in the web browser address bar of the site being used. These are:

- Look for "https" at the start of a website address rather than "http". The "s" stands for "secure" and indicates that the website has security settings in place to protect online payments, by using encryption to ensure as much as possible so that the data cannot be compromised.

Beware

Always be careful of online reviews on retail websites, as a proportion of them have been shown to be fake. As a general rule, disregard the very good and very bad reviews, as the truth may lie somewhere in between.

- To the left of the "https" prefix, there should be a padlock icon. This contains details about the site's security settings. Click on the padlock icon to view details of the related settings and functions.

General online shopping security issues

Fake online shopping sites:

- Look out for fake websites. These will try to steal your credit or debit card details when you attempt to buy something on the site. Fake websites often use similar names to established brands, but look at the website address to see if it seems genuine. Also, look for spelling and grammar errors on the site. See page 104 for more information on website security.

- There should be a Contact Us page, or similar. This is frequently located at the bottom of the page, and it should be available from every page on the site. Look at the Contact Us details to see if they seem genuine and use them to see if you get a reply.

- Conduct a web search using the site's name, and/ or if there is a physical address, do a web search for this, to see if there are any search result for it. If there is something wrong with the site, then there will be comments about this.

- Finally, if something seems too good to be true, then it probably is.

Hot tip

Create a "shopping" email address with a webmail site such as Gmail that you can use for registering with online retailers. This way, any marketing emails will go to this address rather than your usual one.

Booking a Vacation

Getting the best online travel deals

Before booking any vacation it is a good idea to open a web browser (see Chapter 5) and look for some deals online. There are numerous websites that cater for everything from all-inclusive vacations to world cruises. Many of these sites offer a range of products, including flights, hotels, package holidays, and car hire. Look around on different sites to find the best offers for your own requirements. Most travel websites have tabs on the top toolbar for selecting different categories – e.g. Flights or Packages – and also text boxes for entering your dates of travel. The result will be displayed according to which category is selected on the top toolbar.

Hot tip

The internet is also a great source of information for health issues before you go on vacation. This can include details about vaccinations that are required or recommended for certain locations, whether the water is safe to drink, and any specific warnings for selected destinations.

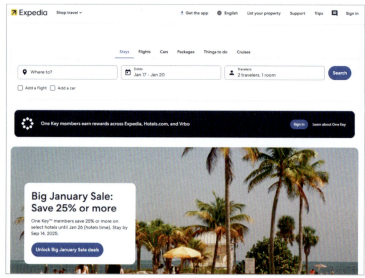

Some websites to look at with the Edge browser to get the best deals are:

- Expedia, at **expedia.com**

- Kayak, at **kayak.com**

- Orbitz, at **orbitz.com**

- Priceline, at **priceline.com**

- Travelocity, at **travelocity.com**

- TravelZoo, at **travelzoo.com**

Booking hotels

As with vacations, there are several websites dedicated to booking hotel rooms around the world. When using these, it is a good idea to find your favorite and stick with this, as you will receive discounts and special offers as you use the site. Hotel websites can be used to find locations around the world and book hotel rooms for selected dates. Also, the search option on these websites can be used to find hotel rooms in specific locations in a city, such as near to a railway station or an airport.

Some online hotel booking websites to look at are **Booking. com**, **Hotels.com**, and **trivago.com**, which is a price comparison website for hotels from different providers.

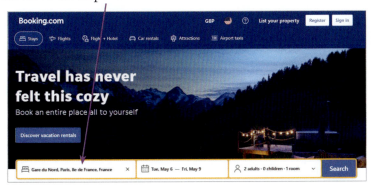

Travel apps

The Microsoft Store has some travel apps that can be used for a variety of purposes. There is no specific Travel category, but the apps can be viewed by entering "travel" into the Microsoft Store Search box.

The app stores for mobile devices (Apple's App Store, and the Google Play Store) have a greater range of travel apps and a specific category for this type of app.

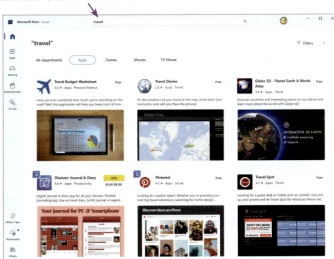

Online Auctions

One of the first great successes of online retailing was auction websites, where items could be bought and sold with a bidding process. The market leader in this was eBay, and this site continues to dominate online auctions, but it has evolved considerably from being just an auction site and now acts as much as a general online retailer, with numerous online retail options where items can be bought and sold without an auction. To use eBay:

Buying items
To buy items on eBay:

1 Access the eBay homepage for your geographic location. Use the top Search box or the category headings to find the item you want to buy

2 Items are displayed for **All listings**, **Auction** or **Buy it now**. Click on the **Auction** button to view items that are for sale with this method

3 For an auction, click on the **Submit bid** button to view the current bidding and the duration of the auction

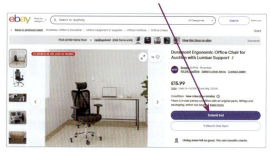

Don't forget

The **Buy it now** option removes any uncertainty when purchasing an item on an auction site, but it also means that there is no negotiation over the price paid.

Selling items

It is now free to list items for sale on eBay, which makes it an even better way of making some money, either as your own business or just to get rid of some items you no longer want. To do this:

1 Click on the **Sell** button on the top toolbar of the eBay homepage and click on the **Sell for free** button

2 Enter details of the item to be sold in the **Start your listing** text box

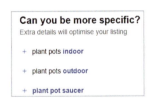

3 As the listing is entered, eBay offers suggestions for refining the listing. Click on an item, as required

4 Check **On** one of the radio buttons to describe the condition of the item

Don't forget

To complete the listing, follow the step-by-step process to add a description of the item, add photos, and specify whether the item is for auction, or choose the **Buy it now** option.

5 Click on the **Continue to listing** button to complete the listing process (see the tip)

Don't forget

Word is part of the Microsoft 365 suite of apps, available by subscription. In some cases, Windows 11 PCs and laptops may come with this pre-installed. See pages 183-184 for details about Microsoft 365.

Hot tip

Some of the Microsoft 365 suite of apps (including Word and Excel) can be accessed, for free, online. To do this, open the page microsoft.com/en-us/microsoft-365/free-office-online-for-the-web in the Edge browser, and click on the **Sign in** button to sign in with your Microsoft Account details (or click on the **Sign up for free** button to create an account). This will provide access to the online Microsoft 365 apps.

Writing Letters

Although handwritten letter writing may be becoming something of a lost art, it is still alive and well in the digital world. There are several word-processing apps that can be used for letter writing, but Microsoft's own Word is one of the best there is partly due to the extensive range of templates for a variety of writing tasks, including letter writing. To create your own letters with Word:

1 Access the **Start** menu and click on the **Word** app

2 Open Word and click on the **More templates** option (a blank document can also be opened)

3 A selection of letter templates is displayed. Click on one to select it

4 Details about the selected template are displayed. Click on the **Create** button to use the template as the basis for your new letter

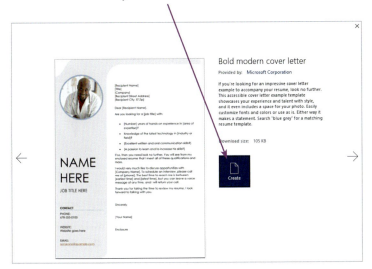

Many of the Word templates have to be downloaded before they can be used, for which an active internet connection is required.

143

5 The new letter, based on the selected template, opens in the Word interface, where it can be customized and formatted – see pages 144-145

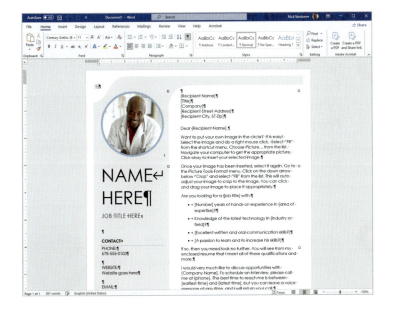

For a detailed look at Microsoft 365 and its apps, see **Microsoft 365 in easy steps, Microsoft Word in easy steps**, and **Microsoft Excel in easy steps** at **www.ineasysteps.com**

144

...cont'd

Formatting a letter

All aspects of Word templates can be customized, while keeping the overall appearance of the document. For a letter template, the first item to customize should be the placeholder image, if there is one. To do this:

1 Right-click on the image and select the **Fill** option

To create the correct proportions for a new image, select it and click on the **Picture Format** option on the top Ribbon. Click on the **Crop** option and select **Fill**.

2 Click on the **Picture...** option

The image is adjusted to fill the image placeholder in the correct proportions.

3 Select an option for inserting an image (the **From a File** option enables you to select an image from your computer)

Insert Pictures

From a File
Browse files on your computer or local network

Stock Images
Unleash your imagination with premium content from the stock image library

Online Pictures
Search images from online sources like Bing, Flickr or OneDrive

From Icons
Search the icon collection

4 The selected image replaces the current one in the image placeholder

To select and format text in a letter:

1 Click in a text box (with square brackets) to select all of the text inside it, or

¶
[Recipient Name]¶
[Title]¶
[Company]¶
[Recipient Street Address]¶
[Recipient City, ST Zip]¶

2 Drag over text that is not in a text box to select it

Dear [Recipient Name],¶

Want to put your own image in the circle? It is easy!
Select the image and do a right mouse click. Select "Fill"
from the shortcut menu. Choose Picture... from the list.
Navigate your computer to get the appropriate picture.
Click okay to insert your selected image.¶

3 Click on the **Home** tab on the top Ribbon

Home

4 Use these options to format the text for items such as font, size, color, bold, italics, and underlining

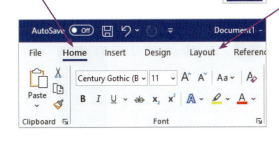

5 Use these options to add bulleted or numbered lists, and indent text and position it to the left, right, or center

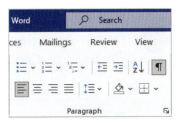

6 Use these options to apply predesigned styles to the selected text

The items on the top Ribbon contain all of the elements needed to format and design a Word document. Click on the main headings on the top toolbar to access the different categories of options.

There are also some excellent free productivity apps that can be downloaded from the web. These include LibreOffice and FreeOffice.

Household Budgets

Keeping track of household accounts and budgets can be a tiresome business. However, with the help of an Excel spreadsheet, it can be made a whole lot easier. To do this:

1 Access the **Start** menu and click on the **Excel** app

2 Open Excel and click on the **More templates** option (a blank spreadsheet can also be opened)

3 A selection of spreadsheet templates is displayed. Click on one to select it; e.g. **Household monthly budget**

4 Details about the selected template are displayed. Click on the **Create** button to use the template as the basis for your new spreadsheet

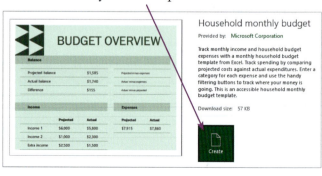

Don't forget

Excel is part of the Microsoft 365 suite of apps, available by subscription. In some cases, Windows 11 PCs and laptops may come with this pre-installed. See pages 183-184 for details about Microsoft 365.

5 The new spreadsheet, based on the selected template, opens in the Excel interface, with the spreadsheet cells populated with the budget details. Each cell can consist of text, numbers or formulae for working out the budget information

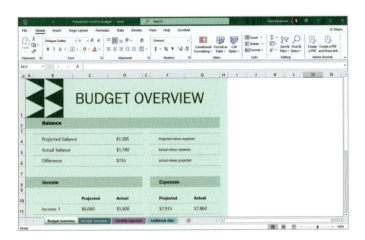

There are numerous elements to Excel and it can take a bit of time and practice to become familiar with using it. For a comprehensive guide to Excel, have a look at Microsoft Excel in easy steps at www.ineasysteps.com

6 Click in a cell to view its contents displayed here. Enter content into this box, as required, to change the item in the cell

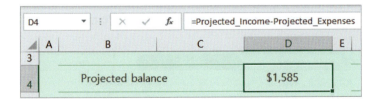

7 The items on the top Ribbon can be used to add content to the spreadsheet and format it, too

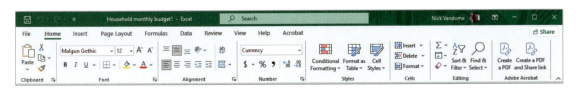

Printing Photos Online

While it is perfectly possible to print photos at home on a color printer, it can be a lot easier and more cost-effective to use one of the numerous online printing services that are available. Search online to find an appropriate online printing service in your region. Most online printing services operate in a similar way.

Online printing websites offer an extensive range of options for your photos, with calendars being one of the most popular.

When the size of print is increased, the quality of the photo may be compromised. If this is the case, a warning message will be displayed. It is still possible to continue with a print at this size, but the quality may be inferior.

1 Once you have registered on a site, upload your photos from your computer, using the **Upload photos** option

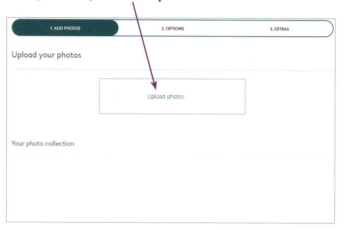

2 To get prints of the uploaded photos, select the size and quantity and carry out any editing that is required, and click on the **Finish Your Order** button

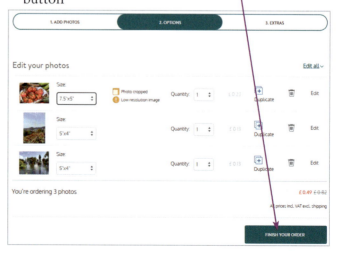

(8) Windows 11 Apps

The emphasis is now on Universal apps in Windows 11. Some are supplied at installation, and there are also many Universal apps in the Microsoft Store, where you can search, review descriptions, then download and install apps on your system for a variety of uses.

Sources for Apps

Although Windows Classic applications are supported, the main functions are provided by Universal apps in Windows 11. As already discussed (see pages 34-43), these can run full-screen or windowed and can use Windows **Snap Layouts** to allow two or more apps to share the screen.

Don't forget

In the past, Windows applications have been available from many sources, including supplier and enthusiast websites, as well as Microsoft. Sources for Windows apps are now much more limited.

The primary design point for the Universal app is the touchscreen, as exemplified by the tablet PC, but all the apps can also be operated on a system with standard monitor, a mouse, and keyboard equipment.

The Windows apps that are available can be found in just two places:

- Supplied and installed with Windows 11.

This is a typical Start menu for a Windows 11 system, showing some of the Windows apps you may expect to find pinned to the Start menu.

- Via the Microsoft Store, where you can find ranges of free apps and paid apps to download and install.

The variety of Universal apps available at the Microsoft Store will change frequently as new products are added and existing products are revised or removed.

Beware

All Universal apps must be submitted to Microsoft for certification before they are allowed in the Microsoft Store (or included on installation discs).

Items submitted to Microsoft can also include Classic apps. These are conventional applications that are listed in the Microsoft Store, but provided from the manufacturer's website via a link that is included with the application description. These, and other conventional apps, may still be obtained directly, without visiting the Microsoft Store.

Supplied with Windows 11

To see which apps have been provided on your system:

1 Select **Settings** > **Apps**

2 Select **Installed apps** to list your apps

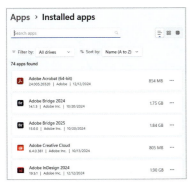
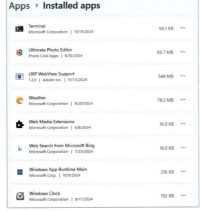

The apps are listed alphabetically. Drag the scroll bar or rotate the scroll wheel on your mouse to see all the apps that are installed.

On the following pages, we will look at the **Calculator**, **Clock**, and **Weather** apps. We also review the Microsoft Store and the app categories that it offers and discuss the Search options that help you locate apps related to specific topics.

Other apps, such as **Mail**, **Calendar**, **Microsoft Edge**, **Photos**, and the various games apps, will be discussed in the relevant chapters on the specific topics.

Another way to list all the apps on your system is to left-click the **Start** button and then click the **All** button.

All the apps will be listed, and this list will be preceded by a list of **Most used** apps.

You can pin any of these apps onto the Start menu so that they appear in the **Pinned** area (see page 61).

Calculator

While it is no substitute for a full spreadsheet application, the Windows **Calculator** app provides quite powerful computational facilities.

1 Select the **Calculator** app from the **All** list on the Start menu

2 In **Standard** mode, type or click to enter a calculation using the desired operation symbol, and press = to display the result

Click the function buttons or press the equivalent keyboard keys (see the first tip) to perform addition, subtraction, multiplication, division, square root, percentage and inverse operations. You can also store and recall numbers from memory, and the **History** capability keeps track of stages in the calculations.

In addition to **Standard** mode, there are also **Scientific** and **Programmer** modes, plus a variety of **Converter** options provided.

1 Open **Calculator**, then click the **Menu** button to list the modes

2 Select **Scientific** to see the features it offers

Scientific mode gives a variety of logarithmic, trigonometric, and factorial functions in various forms, such as degrees, radians, etc.

You can also use the numeric keypad on your keyboard to type numbers and operators. Press the **Num Lock** key if it is not already turned **On**.

You will also find a large number of equivalent apps at the Microsoft Store if you search for the term "calculator".

3 Select **Programmer** mode to see what it has to offer

The **Programmer** calculator operates in decimal, hexadecimal, octal, and binary formats. It supports byte, word, dword, and qword. There's a full keypad, including alphabetics for hex numbers, and an alternative bit-toggling keypad.

Unlike the other **Calculator** modes, **Programmer** mode does not maintain a history of computations.

4 From the **Converter** options, select a category – for example, **Weight and mass** – and choose **From** and **To** units; e.g. **Kilograms** to **Pounds**

Note how the converter suggests some equivalents, in related units – in this example, the number of soccer balls.

Each of the categories offers a range of appropriate units, and they all suggest equivalents to your results, sometimes quite idiosyncratic in nature.

5 Switch to the **Energy** category to convert between **Food calories** and **Joules**

6 Enter 2456 as the starting value

You are told that this quantity of energy is about equal to 2.33 BTUs (British Thermal Units).

There are 13 different **Converter** options, each with a range of units.

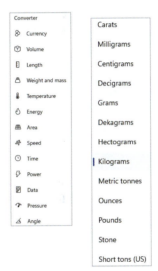

The **Weight and mass** category offers a total of 14 different units that you can convert to and from. Scroll down to see the final option, **Long tons (UK)**.

153

Clock

The **Clock** app is a combination of **World Clock**, **Alarm Clock**, **Stopwatch**, and **Timer**. You can use it to set alarms and reminders, to check the time anywhere in the world, and to time your activities.

1 Select **Clock** from **All** and click the **Menu** button. (You may be asked to enter your Microsoft Account password)

2 Select any of the four types of clock to review its features

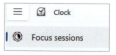

3 Select **Focus sessions** to create a period of time when you are not disturbed by notifications

Weather

This app displays forecasts of temperature, wind direction and speed, humidity, etc. for your default or chosen location.

1 Select **Weather** from the Start menu to see an overview for the current day

The **Weather** app also runs on tablets and adjusts itself to suit their particular screen sizes.

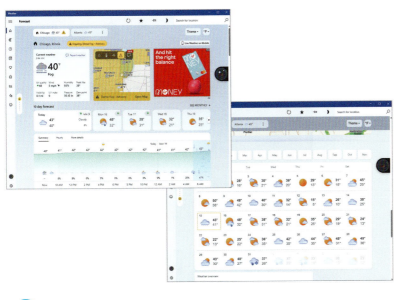

2 Choose a later date if desired, then view the forecast, selecting either **Summary, Hourly**, or **Details**

3 Scroll down in any view to see details for the specified day, including historical peaks and averages

Click the buttons on the **Icon bar** to display maps, historical weather, and favorite locations. Click the **Menu** button to show the titles of icons.

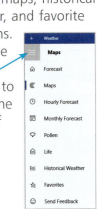

Microsoft Store

The **Microsoft Store** recognizes which version of Windows your system is running and displays apps appropriate for you. To see what's offered:

1 Click the **Microsoft Store** icon on the Start menu or on the Taskbar to open the Store at the homepage

2 You will see several highlighted apps

3 Scroll down to view more categories – e.g. **Best selling apps**

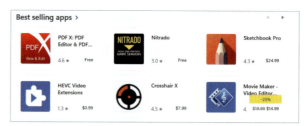

4 Click the right-pointing arrowhead next to the group name to display all items in the group

Best selling apps >

Hot tip

The **Microsoft Store** is the source for new Universal apps for your Windows 11 system and is organized to help you identify useful items.

5 The items in the selected group are displayed

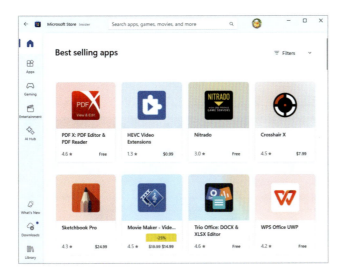

The **Microsoft Store** can display all types of items with **Home** selected, or you can restrict it to **Apps**, **Gaming**, **Entertainment**, or **AI Hub**.

6 Click on the **Filters** button for options for which items are displayed

≡ Filters ∧

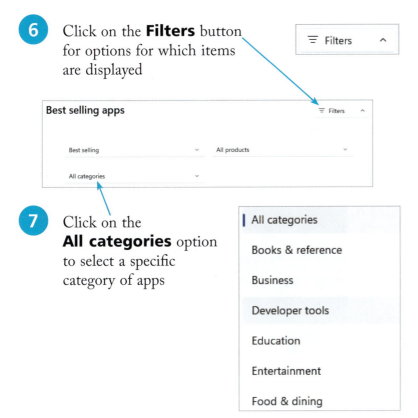

7 Click on the **All categories** option to select a specific category of apps

Collections

The **Collections** section can be accessed from the Home section in the Microsoft Store – scroll down to the bottom of these pages to see Collections, which include:

Creativity apps
These can be used for a range of creativity tasks, such as drawing and photo editing.

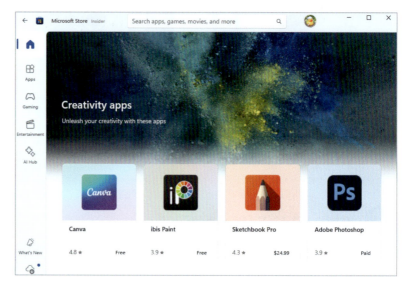

Personalization apps
These can be used for a selection of personalization options for your Windows 11 computer, including themes and wallpaper.

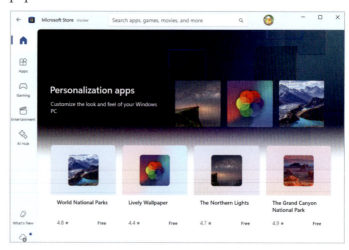

The **Collections** section is accessed by clicking on the right-pointing arrowhead next to **Collections**, when you scroll down the **Home** section of the Microsoft Store.

158

Within the Collections section are **Windows themes**, **Racing games**, **Creativity apps**, **Games for kids**, **Social networking apps**, **Getting started**, **Productivity apps**, and **Personalization apps**.

Searching the Microsoft Store

You can use the Search box found on the Microsoft Store screen to find items of interest.

1 Select the Search box and type a search term – for example, "aquatic"

2 The top few matches are displayed immediately

3 Click the magnifying glass icon to show all the results

Don't forget

You may not be sure of the exact name of the app you need, but you can search the Microsoft Store using a descriptive term to identify the app.

159

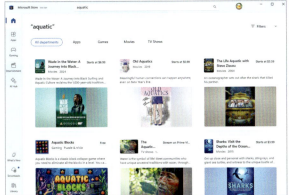

You will be shown results for all departments, and you can then choose to view an individual grouping – **Apps**, **Games**, **Movies**, or **TV Shows**.

4 Select the **Apps** button to list apps related to your search term

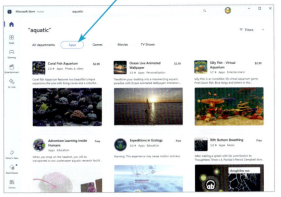

Installing Apps

1 Find an app you want to investigate; for example, **PDF X: Editor & PDF Reader**

2 If you decide you want this app on your system, click the **Get** button

During the process, messages from the Microsoft Store let you know the progress of actions being performed.

3 The app is downloaded and installed. Click the **Open** button to launch the app, or

4 You will find an entry for the app in the **All** list, with a **New** label

5 Right-click the **All** entry and select **Pin to Start** to add it to the **Pinned** section of the Start menu

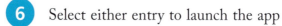

6 Select either entry to launch the app

Apps can be pinned to the Taskbar by right-clicking on them in the **All** section of the Start menu and selecting **More** > **Pin to taskbar**.

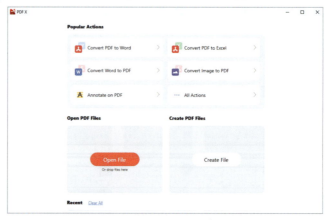

Your Microsoft Account

From the Microsoft Store, you can go to your Microsoft Account to list the devices and apps that have been installed for this account.

1 Open the **Microsoft Store** app and click the **Profile** button in the top-right corner, then select **Manage account and devices**

2 **Microsoft Edge** opens the web page for your Microsoft Account, to which you have to sign in

3 Scroll down to display the devices that are associated with this account

4 Scroll on down to access further details of your Microsoft Account

You can review your privacy settings, access security tools, manage payment options, and review the order history for your Microsoft Account.

Don't forget

You can choose to personalize the account by adding a profile photo that will appear on apps and devices that use the Microsoft Account.

161

Updates

If any Universal app that you've installed gets updated, the changes are supplied through the Microsoft Store. In Windows 11, these updates are applied automatically in the background, without any notification, by default.

If you'd prefer to manually accept and install updates:

1 Open the **Microsoft Store** app, click the **Profile** icon and select **Settings**

2 Click the button for **App updates**, to turn off automatic updating

When you drag an option button, it will change color from the accent color (**On**) to white (**Off**) or vice versa, to indicate the changed status.

3 The setting for **App updates** is reversed

4 To view the update status, select **Library** from the sidebar on the **App settings** panel, to find a list of downloaded and installed apps

Scroll on down to see a full list of items for your account. These can include **Apps**, **Games**, and **Movies & TV**.

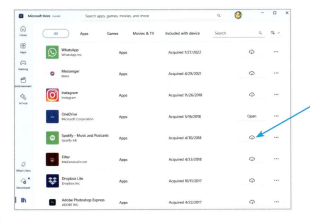

Items may be flagged with a cloud icon. This means that the item is available online but is not currently installed on your device. Click the icon to initiate the installation.

Select a group – **Games**, for example – to list its contents.

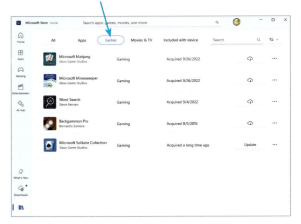

Select any of the entries listed to check its status on the current device.

If you already own a game but it's not present on the current device, you will see an **Install** button. If the game is installed, you will see a **Play** button.

Verifying your Identity

It is possible to verify your Microsoft Account so that details from it can be synchronized online and across different devices for the same account. To do this:

1 Open the **Settings** app and click on the **Accounts** category in the left-hand sidebar

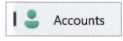

2 Click on the **Your info** option

3 Click on the **Verify** button

Don't forget

You can select either an email address or a telephone number, depending on what contact information is in the profile for your Microsoft Account.

Account settings

⚠ Verify your identity to sync passwords across your devices.   Verify

4 Click on the email address used for the Microsoft Account. An email will be sent to this account

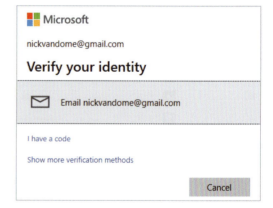

5 Enter the code sent in the email and click on the **Verify** button to verify your Microsoft Account

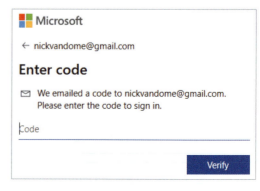

Authenticator App

The **Microsoft Authenticator** app can be used if you need to verify your Microsoft Account when you are logging in to it. This can be done from a mobile device, such as a tablet or a smartphone, giving an additional layer of security. It can also be used to access non-Microsoft accounts online. To obtain and use the app:

1 Visit the app store for your mobile device; an iPad, for example

2 Search the app store for "microsoft authenticator"

Hot tip

This illustrates adding the **Microsoft Authenticator** app for an iPad. A similar process will be needed to add the equivalent app for your smartphone.

165

3 Select **Get** and then select **Install** for the **Microsoft Authenticator** app, to add it to your mobile device

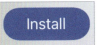

4 Tap on the **Microsoft Authenticator** app on your mobile device to open it

...cont'd

The app is now ready for you to add the Microsoft Accounts you may need to verify.

Hot tip

You can be added as a new user to any Windows 11 device and use your Microsoft Account to sign in to that device.

Hot tip

The next time you need to verify your identity, it will call upon the **Microsoft Authenticator** app, and you can approve the request on your mobile device.

1. Click **Add account** to start validating your Microsoft Account

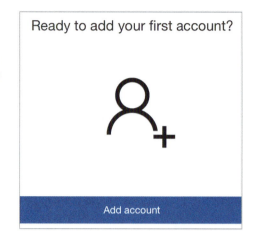

Ready to add your first account?

Add account

2. Follow prompts to sign in to the Microsoft Account and click on the email address used for the account

Microsoft

nickvandome@mac.com

Verify your identity

✉ Email nickvandome@mac.com

I have a code

I don't have any of these

Cancel

3. A verification code is sent to the email address selected in Step 2. Enter this into the authenticator and tap on the **Verify** button

Microsoft

← nickvandome@mac.com

Enter code

✉ We emailed a code to nickvandome@mac.com. Please enter the code to sign in.

Code

Cancel   Verify

9 Outlook for Email and More

Windows 11 provides the Outlook app for email, address book, and calendar functions. The Chat option within Teams can also be used for text and video chats.

About Outlook

With the latest version of Windows 11, the Outlook app is used for email, calendar, and address book functions. All of them can be accessed from the same app rather than separate apps as in previous versions of Windows. To get started with Outlook:

168

1 Click on the **Outlook** app on the Start menu

Outlook (new)

2 Select your Microsoft Account details in the **Suggested accounts** box (or click on the **Create an Outlook. com email account** link)

Welcome to the new Outlook

Outlook supports Microsoft 365, Gmail, Yahoo, iCloud, IMAP, and POP. Learn More

Suggested accounts ⓘ

nickvandome@googlemail.com ⌄

No account? Create an Outlook.com email account

3 Click on the **Continue** button

Troubleshooting | Continue | Advanced Setup

4 Click on the **Apply Settings** button to use the settings that have already been applied in the Windows 11 settings for language, time, and themes

Let's make Outlook familiar

N nickvandome@googlemail.com

We'll apply your language, time, and theme settings from Windows. This one-time process will also update the same settings in Outlook on the web. Learn more.

Apply Settings | Skip

5 Once you have signed in, the icons in the left-hand sidebar can be used to access the various Outlook apps. By default, Outlook opens at the **Mail** option

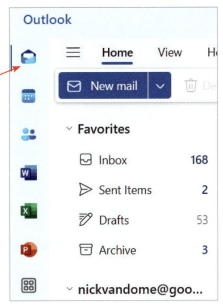

Outlook settings

The Outlook app has a number of settings that can be applied to the app itself and the elements within it.

1 Click on this button on the top toolbar to access the range of settings

2 Click on **Accounts** in the left-hand sidebar to view details about the account that is using the Outlook app. Click on the **Add account** button to include another account

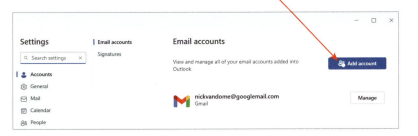

169

...cont'd

3 Click on **General** in the left-hand sidebar to view details about how the Outlook app operates

4 Click on items to the right of the left-hand sidebar to view more options for the selected category; for instance, general **Appearance** options for the Outlook app

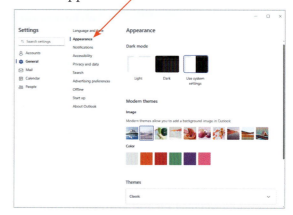

The **Appearance** option in Step 4 is applied to the background of the Outlook app, regardless of which section is being used.

5 Another useful option in the **General** section is the **Privacy and data** category, for security settings

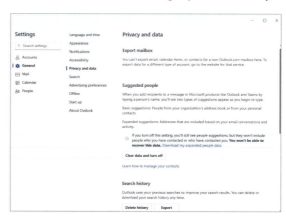

6 Click on **Mail** in the left-hand sidebar to view settings for using this section of Outlook

7 The **Mail** option has a useful secondary level of menu items, for managing its functions

8 Click on **Calendar** in the left-hand sidebar to view settings for using this section of Outlook

9 Click on **People** in the left-hand sidebar to view settings for using this section of Outlook

The **People** section in the Outlook settings only has two options, for displaying contacts by first or last name.

The Mail Window

These are the main elements of the **Mail** window:

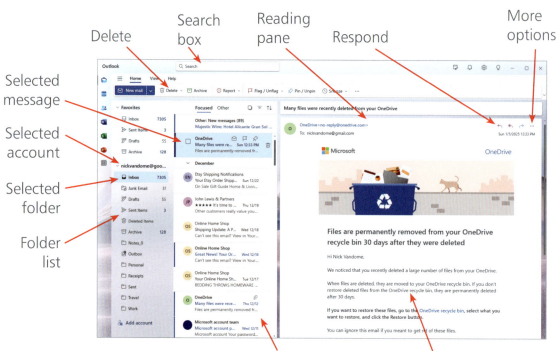

Delete Search box Reading pane Respond More options

Selected message

Selected account

Selected folder

Folder list

Folder (Inbox) pane Message contents

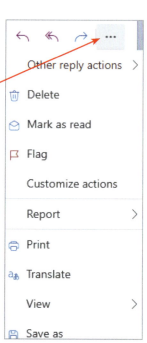

1 Click **More options (...)** at the top right of the window to display commands for dealing with messages in your Mailbox

Viewing Messages

1 Select a message from the **Folder** pane, and it displays in the **Reading** pane

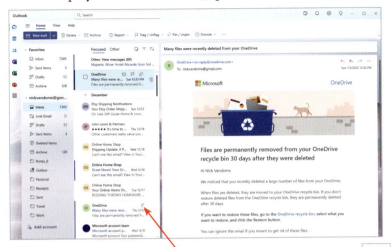

Don't forget

Pictures can be included in the body of email messages, as well as saved from them. Other files such as documents can also be sent, saved, or opened from a message.

2 If there is an attachment with a message (indicated by a paperclip icon), it will be contained within the email body or shown as a link

3 Click **Reply** to respond to the sender, **Reply all** for all addressees, or **Forward** to send to another person

← Reply   ← Reply all   → Forward

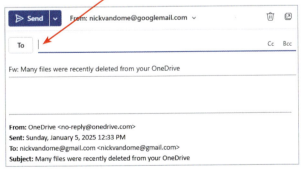

Hot tip

You can add recipients from the **All contacts** list of the People section of the Outlook app; see pages 176-177.

4 Type your reply and click the **Send** button when finished

5 A copy is saved in the **Sent items** folder of the account used to send the reply

173

Creating a Message

1 In **Mail**, select an email account, go to the Inbox and click the **New mail** button (or press **Ctrl** + **N**)

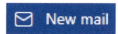

2 A blank message is displayed, ready for recipient details and content

When entering contact names in the **To:** box, you may see several suggestions that match so far, but the number reduces as you enter more of the name.

3 Type in the email address of the recipient, or choose their name from the list that appears if you have already added their contact details to the **People** section of Outlook – see pages 176-177

To attach an item to an email, click the **Insert** tab on the top toolbar (see Step 9 on the next page) and choose an option from **File**, **Table**, **Pictures**, **Link**, and **Emoji**.

4 Add more recipients in the same way, selecting from the suggestions where appropriate

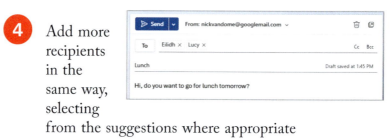

5 Click in the **Add a subject** box and type text for the title of the message

6 Click in the body of the message and add a salutation and message text

7 Select **Cc & Bcc** to add boxes for recipients who will be copied in on the email

8 You can format the text in your message if you wish – click the **Format text** tab

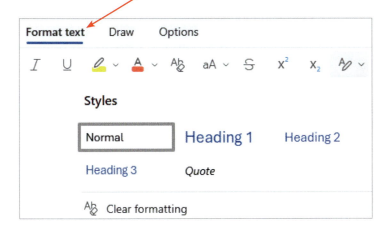

9 There are also font formatting and paragraph formatting options, including an option for adding **Pictures**, from the **Insert** tab

10 Navigate to an image, as required, click on it to select it, then click the **Open** button to add it to a message

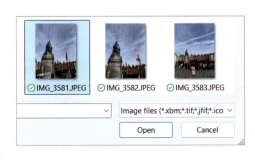

11 Click the **Send** button to send the message

Hot tip

Recipients added using **Bcc** (Blind carbon-copy) will not be shown on copies of the message that others receive. Recipients added using **Cc** will see all other recipients included in the email.

Don't forget

Sometimes, a message to an email address may fail, perhaps because the email service is offline for a period. After several attempts, an error response message may be returned to you. An email might also fail because you've entered the wrong email address, so double-check spellings and whether .com/.co etc. at the end of the email address is correct.

175

People Option

An electronic address book is always a good feature to have on a computer, and with Windows 11 this function is provided by the **People** option in Outlook. This not only allows you to add your own contacts manually; you can also link to any of your online accounts – such as Gmail or iCloud – and import the contacts that you have there.

Adding contacts

The first step is to add contacts to the **People** section.

1 Open Outlook and click on this icon in the left-hand sidebar

2 Click on the **New contact** button at the top of the **People** window

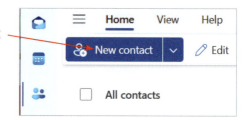

3 Enter details for the new contact, including name, email address, and phone number

4 Click on the **Add [item]** button next to a category to add another field for that category

Hot tip

Once a contact has been added, select it from the **All contacts** section, as shown on the next page, and click on the **Edit** button at the top of the sidebar to edit the contact's details.

| ✎ Edit | 🗑 Delete |

5 Click on the **Add name field** option at the top of the new contact window to add a new category within the window

6 Click on the **Save** button at the bottom of the window to create a new contact

Finding people

To find people that have been added:

1 Click on the **All contacts** option to view all of the contacts that have been added in the **People** section

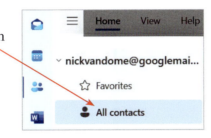

2 Click on a letter heading below **All contacts** to access an alphabetic grid

3 Click on a letter in the alphabetic grid to go to that heading in the **All contacts** list

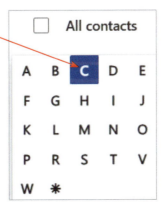

Hot tip

Click on the **Sort by** option to the right of the **All contacts** heading to select options for how entries are displayed.

Hot tip

To delete a contact, right-click on their name in the **All contacts** list and click on the **Delete** button to remove them.

177

Using the Calendar

The **Calendar** option in Outlook can be used to record important events and add reminders. To view the calendar:

1 Open Outlook and click on this icon in the left-hand sidebar

2 Click here to view the calendar in **Day**, **Work Week**, **Week**, or **Month** mode

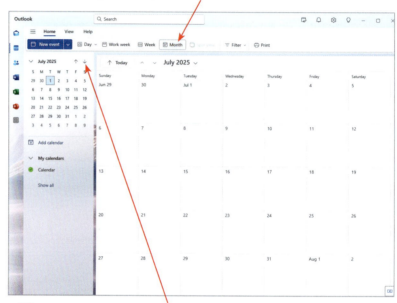

Hot tip

Click on the **Work week** option in Step 2 to access options for displaying the calendar as a work week – i.e. five days (Monday to Friday) – or a full week.

3 Click on these buttons to move between months (or swipe left or right on a touchpad)

4 Click on the menu button at the top of the Outlook window to show or hide the navigation pane, which includes a minimized version of the calendar

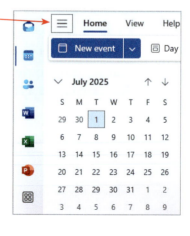

Adding events

Events can be added to the calendar, and various settings can be applied to them, such as recurrence and reminders.

1 Click on a date to create a new event, and click on the **New event** button

2 Enter a title at the top of the window

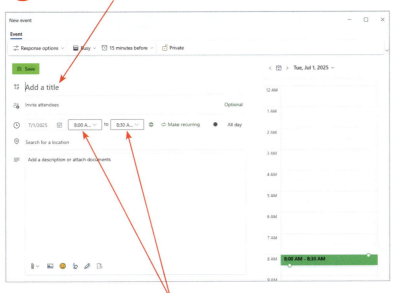

3 Click here and select a time for the start and end of the event. If **All day** is selected, the time fields will not be available

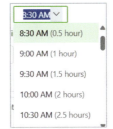

4 Use these options at the top of the **Event** window to, from left to right: request responses to an event; show your availability; set an alarm for the event; or make the event private

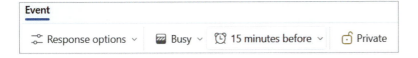

Click on the **Save** button at the top of the new event window to save the event and add it to your calendar.

179

Teams and Chat

Windows 11 is integrated closely with the Microsoft Teams collaboration and communication app. Part of this is the chat function, which provides text and video chat options. To get started with Teams and Chat:

1 Click on the **Microsoft Teams** app on the Start menu

If the Microsoft Teams app is not already on your computer, it can be downloaded from the Microsoft Store.

2 Click here to select your own Microsoft Account for using Teams

3 Enter the name you want to appear for Teams and Chat and click on the **Continue** button

For a detailed look at Microsoft Teams, see Microsoft Teams in easy steps at www.ineasysteps.com

4 To verify your account, you will be emailed an access code to your Microsoft Account email address. Enter the code and click on the **Verify** button

5 Click on the **New chat** button to start a new text or video conversation using the chat function

6 Click in the **To:** box to enter the details of a contact with whom you want to conduct a chat

To: Enter name, email or phone number

7 Click on this button to start a new text chat. Click on the video icon to start a video chat

Chat

8 Click in the **Type a message** box to start creating a text message. Use the icons below the box to, from left to right: add emojis, GIFs, and stickers; add a photo; add a file as an attachment; other actions and apps (**+** icon); or send the message

Type a message

Hot tip

If you have an Android smartphone, this can be linked to Teams and the chat function, by clicking on the **Link your phone** button in Step 5 and following the step-by-step process.

Link your phone

181

Don't forget

Depending on how you have entered your contacts, you may be able to enter the start of someone's name in the **To:** box in Step 6 to select them from your existing contacts, or you may need to enter their full details; i.e. their email address.

...cont'd

9 Click on the **Emoji** icon in Step 8 on page 181 and click on an emoji to add it to the text message. Click on the toolbar at the bottom of the panel, to access different categories of emojis, GIFs and stickers

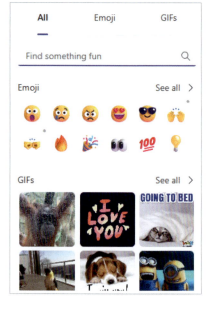

10 When a conversation is created with the chat window, it continues down the screen as messages are added

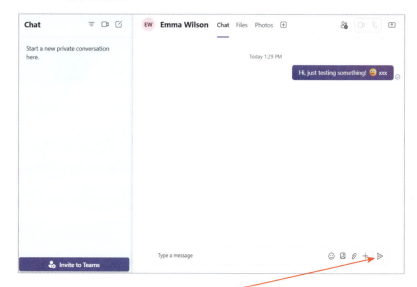

11 Click on this button in the bottom right-hand corner of the chat window to send a message

Microsoft 365

Previously known as Microsoft Office, Microsoft 365 is a suite of productivity apps that can be used for tasks such as word processing and creating spreadsheets and presentations. It is a subscription service, with the apps being downloaded from the Microsoft website. To access Microsoft 365 and get started with it:

1 Go to **microsoft.com/en-us/microsoft-365** to view details about the versions of Microsoft 365. Click on the **For home** button

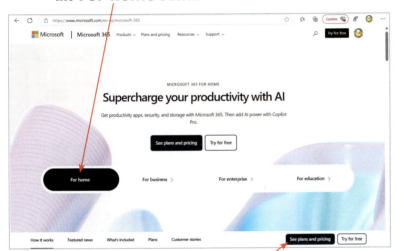

If you have a tablet or smartphone, you can search the Microsoft Store to find free mobile versions of **Word**, **PowerPoint**, and **Excel**. There are also free online versions of these (see page 142).

2 Click on the **See plans and pricing** button to view the subscription options for Microsoft 365

...cont'd

3   Go to **microsoft.com/en-us/microsoft-365/free-office-online-for-the-web** to view details about how the Microsoft 365 apps can be used for free, on the web and on mobile devices

You need to sign in online with your Microsoft Account details in order to use the free apps on the web and on mobile devices.

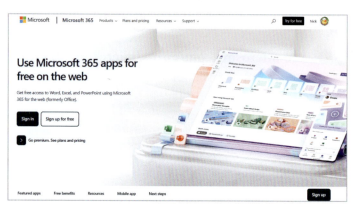

Microsoft 365 apps

The apps that are available with Microsoft 365 are Word, Excel, PowerPoint, Outlook, Teams, OneNote, ClipChamp, and OneDrive.

Word, Excel, and PowerPoint are the main productivity apps in Microsoft 365, and they all have ranges of templates that can be used as a starting point for creating documents:

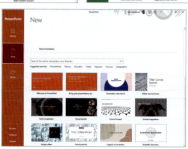

10 Windows Games

There are some great games that you can play on a Windows 11 computer, and the Xbox app can be used to play and access games, too.

Games in Windows 11

There are a limited number of games pre-installed with Windows 11, including **Microsoft Solitaire Collection**. However, you will find many games available in the Microsoft Store, from the **Gaming** tab in the left-hand sidebar. These include many free games, though you should be aware that associated in-game purchases may be suggested during play.

Xbox is Microsoft's video game console, competing with Sony's PlayStation. The Xbox network service allows players to play games online via a broadband connection.

Scroll down the page to see a full selection of available games, or click on the right-pointing arrowhead next to a category heading, or scroll through the options with the arrows at the right-hand side.

Microsoft has integrated Xbox content and gaming services into Windows 11 and provides the **Xbox** app (see page 196).

This gives Windows 11 players access to the Xbox network so that they can keep track of their achievements, see what their friends are playing, and be participators in multiplayer games.

Xbox console users are also able to stream their Xbox games to their Windows 11 PC or tablet.

Games in the Microsoft Store

To get started with games from the Microsoft Store:

1 Click on the **Microsoft Store** icon on the Taskbar

2 Click on the **Gaming** icon in the left-hand sidebar to access the Gaming homepage within the Microsoft Store

3 Scroll down to see a selection of **Best selling games**. Best sellers include free as well as chargeable games. The Microsoft Store also identifies games you have installed

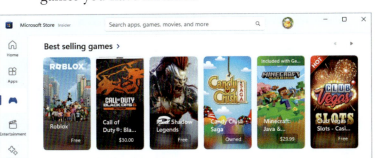

4 Scroll down to find a selection of **Top paid games**

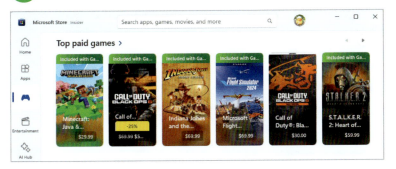

Don't forget

The games that are featured and the games selected for each list will change frequently, but these examples illustrate the types of findings you can expect.

...cont'd

5 Scroll on, using the vertical scroll bar or the mouse wheel, and review a selection of **Top free games** (and click the right-pointing arrowhead to explore the complete set)

6 You can also explore the various **Collections** of games or view a selection of **Games specials**

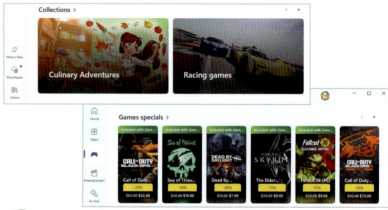

Hot tip

Individual games may appear in several groups. For example, games shown in the **Top free** or **Top paid** selections may also be included in the **Collections** selection.

7 Some categories have a **Filters** button – click in the **All categories** box to view all of the available games categories

Word Games

1 Go to the Microsoft Store and search for games under the term "word search"

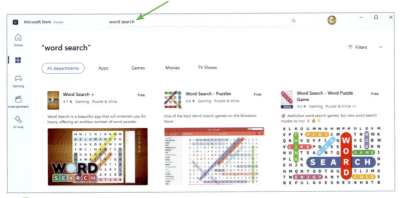

2 Select an app from the search results, and follow the prompts to install it on your system

3 Open the app to start a new word search game. Drag over the required words on the screen to select them

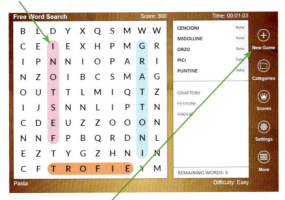

4 Select **New Game** and choose the difficulty level

Don't forget

You can choose games that are complex and challenging, such as **Mahjong** and **Solitaire**, or you can choose simple games that are easy and fun to play.

Microsoft Solitaire Collection

If you have enjoyed playing **FreeCell** or **Spider Solitaire** in a previous release of Windows, you'll be pleased to find **Microsoft Solitaire Collection** in the Store.

By signing in and creating an Xbox profile (see page 196), you can record the results for all the games you play and share your achievements with other players.

1 Find the game in the Microsoft Store and note if it is already installed on your system

2 Select the Store entry to see its description. You are advised that there are in-game purchase options

3 Select **Play** from the Store entry (or select the **Start** menu entry)

4 The app loads up and offers you a choice of **Klondike**, **Spider**, **FreeCell**, **Pyramid**, and **TriPeaks**

5 Click on the **Menu** button in the top left-hand corner to access options for playing the game, including the different game versions

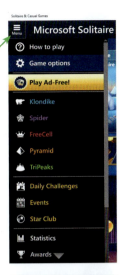

6 Click on the **Game options** item in the previous step to access options for how games operate

7 Select a game as appropriate to start playing it, from the options in Step 4 on the previous page

If you make a disallowed move, a warning box will appear with the appropriate details.

Microsoft Minesweeper

1 Find **Microsoft Minesweeper** in the Microsoft Store to view a description of the game

The process that you follow to install and play **Minesweeper** is typical for games on Windows 11 PCs.

2 Click **Install** and follow the prompts to install the game

3 Select the app from the **All** list on the Start menu to open the game. An introduction screen is displayed before accessing the app's homepage

4 Choose one of the game types such as **Easy 9x9** to get started, or choose a more

advanced level depending on your experience and ability

5 A tutorial option is displayed. Click **Next** to move through the tutorial or **Skip** to close it

6 A board at the selected level is displayed. The first click is safe, but after that you must check before selecting a cell as safe or potentially mined. Each number indicates the number of mines next to it

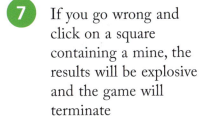

You use the numbers displayed to help deduce whether a square is safe to uncover. Right-click a suspect square to add a flag, or left-click a safe cell. On a touchscreen, you would press and hold for a flag or tap for a safe cell.

7 If you go wrong and click on a square containing a mine, the results will be explosive and the game will terminate

8 Get it right, and you are treated to fireworks at the end of the game and the mines are displayed

9 Your scores are recorded and can be made available to the Xbox app (and your Xbox gamertag – see page 196) so that they can be shared with other players

Microsoft Mahjong

1 Locate the game in the Microsoft Store and click the **Install** button to install it, then pin it to the Start menu if required

This game has four skill levels, with about 24 puzzles for each. It can be played with keyboard, mouse, or by touch.

2 Click on the required icon on the **Start** menu (or select it in the **All** area)

3 Click on the **Themes** button to select an overall theme for the look of the game

4 Select a theme and click on the **OK** button

...cont'd

5 Click on the **Menu** button to access options for playing the game, including the different game versions and a **How to Play** tutorial

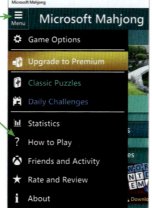

6 Click on the **Menu** button again to exit the menu and select a puzzle to play. Use the tabs at the top of the window to select **Easy**, **Medium**, **Hard**, or **Expert** levels

7 Complete the selected puzzle. Fireworks are displayed when you complete a puzzle, and the next puzzle is then available

The first time you play, you are offered a tutorial to help you learn the basic operations of the game. You can skip the tutorial if you wish.

Xbox App

The Xbox app provides access to Windows 11 versions of Xbox games. You do not have to own an Xbox games device.

1 Click the **Xbox** icon on the Start menu and Xbox opens with your gamertag

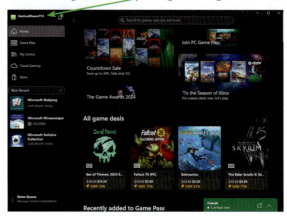

2 Click on your gamertag icon to access menu options for the Xbox app

3 Click on the **Settings** option to view the full range of settings for the Xbox app

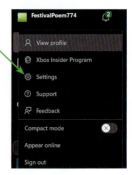

4 Click on the **My Library** option in the sidebar in Step 1 to view your Xbox games and add new ones

11 Music and Pictures

This chapter shows how you can create recordings, play CDs, and add music to the Media Player. You can also manage movie and TV show collections and view and edit your favorite photos.

Sound Card and Speakers

The sound card in your computer processes the information from apps such as **Media Player** and sends audio signals to your computer's speakers.

To review and adjust your sound setup:

1 Click on the **Settings** app on the Taskbar

2 Click on the **System** category in the left-hand sidebar

3 Click on the **Sound** option

4 Select options for sound output as required. Click on the **Speakers** option to view the properties for your computer's speakers

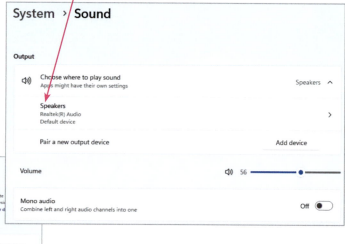

5 Select options for the speakers, including allowing apps to use them, general volume settings and volume settings for the left and right channels

In general, it is best to keep the volume settings at the same level for the left and right channels.

Recording

With a sound card in your system, you can make voice recordings from a microphone or other audio sources. To access settings for your microphone:

1 Access the **Sound** settings as shown on the previous page

2 Select options for sound input as required. Click on the **Microphone** option to view the properties of your computer's microphone, if it has one

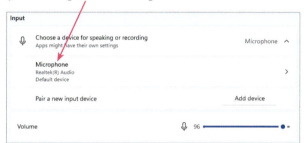

3 Click on the **Microphone test** option to do a sound test for the microphone

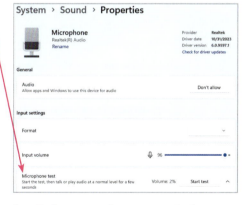

4 On the main **Sound** page, in the **Advanced** section, click on **Troubleshoot common sound problems** for either **Output devices** or **Input devices**

Click on the **More sound settings** option in Step 4 to access more options for individual devices.

Media Player

The **Media Player** app can be used to play and manage digital music with Windows 11. To use it:

1 Select **Media Player** from the Start menu or **All** list

2 The **Media Player** homepage is displayed, with the left-hand sidebar used for navigating around

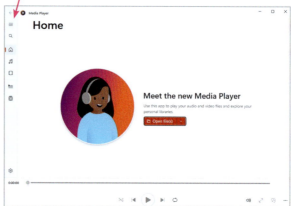

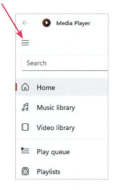

200

3 You may need to add the **Music** folder from your PC to the **Media Player** app, by clicking the **Add folder** button in the **Music library** section

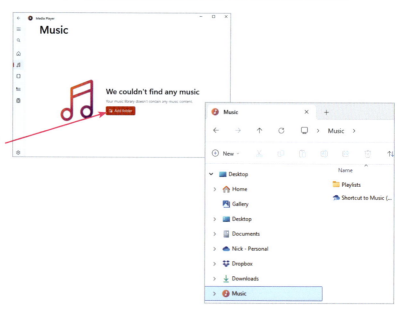

4 Click on **Music library** in the sidebar to choose to list songs, albums, or artists, as shown at the top of the next page. The albums in your Music library will be listed in alphabetical sequence and with cover pictures displayed

Details of the current track are shown, and the progression is illustrated by a slider at the bottom of the window.

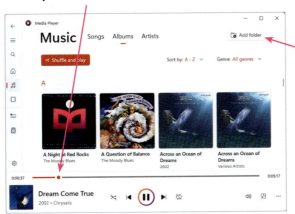

You can click the **Add folder** button to specify another folder that contains music.

For more details about using the **Music library**, see page 205.

see page 205

5 To change the sequence in which albums are displayed, click **Sort by** and then choose an option: **A - Z**, **Release year**, **Artist**, or **Date added**

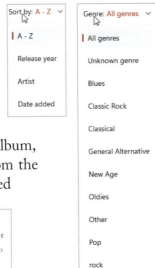

You can play albums that are on your OneDrive on any device where you sign in with your Microsoft Account.

6 To filter the list by type of album, click **Genre** and choose from the extensive list of genres offered

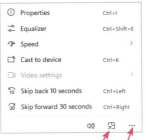

The **Mini player** in Step 7 is a pop-out window that contains the music controls for the **Media Player** so that it can be used when other apps are accessed.

7 You can adjust the volume, switch to the **Mini player**, or select **More options** (**...**) to display a list of actions that are available

201

Playing Audio CDs

Although playing an audio CD on a computer may seem a little old-fashioned in a world of streaming music, it nevertheless plays an important role as there are still many CDs that are used for music. To do this:

1 Insert an audio CD into your computer's CD drive and open the **Media Player** app

2 Click on this button (**Audio CD**) in the left-hand sidebar

3 Details of the audio CD are displayed in the main window

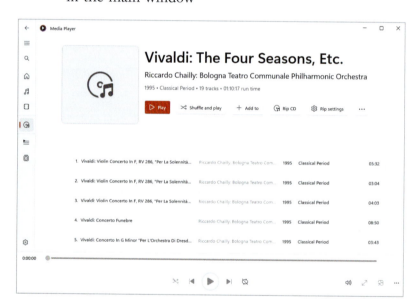

4 Click on a track to select it, then click on the **Play** button

5 Click on the **Shuffle and play** button to play the tracks of the CD in a random order

Beware

Windows 11 PCs and laptops rarely come with an internal CD drive. If you want to play an audio CD, an external CD drive will be required. The Audio CD icon in Step 2 only appears when there is an available CD drive connected to the Windows 11 device.

Hot tip

If you want to copy tracks from an audio CD onto your computer, this can be done with a process called ripping (see page 204 for details).

6 As a track plays, the music controls are available at the bottom of the window

Drag the slider in Step 6 to move to different points in a track.

7 Use these controls to, from left to right: shuffle the tracks on the CD; go to the start of the current track being played; pause or play the current track; go to the end of the current track; and repeat the current track being played

8 Use these controls to, from left to right: change the volume; display the Media Player in full screen; minimize the Media Player window so that it only takes up a small part of the screen; and access the **More options** panel

Be careful not to set the volume too high for an audio CD, particularly for an extended period of time.

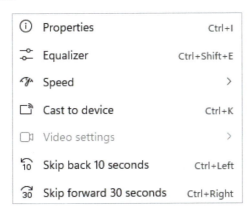

ⓘ Properties	Ctrl+I
⚬ Equalizer	Ctrl+Shift+E
Speed	>
Cast to device	Ctrl+K
Video settings	>
Skip back 10 seconds	Ctrl+Left
Skip forward 30 seconds	Ctrl+Right

203

Copying Tracks

In addition to playing an audio CD with a Windows 11 computer, it is also possible to copy the tracks onto your computer, which is known as ripping. To do this:

1 Insert an audio CD into your computer's CD drive and open the **Media Player** app. Click on the **Audio CD** button, as shown on page 202

2 Click on the **Rip settings** button

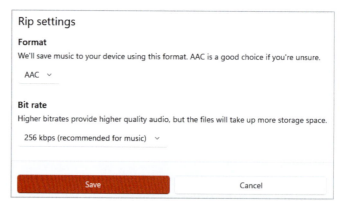

3 Apply settings for copying the CD, as required, and click on the **Save** button

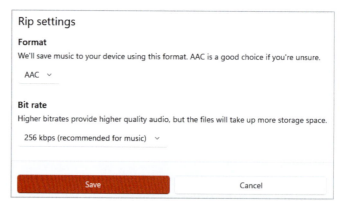

4 Click on the **Rip CD** button to copy the audio tracks to the Media Player app. The progress is shown next to each track

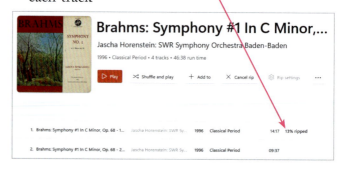

Click on the **Edit info** button in Step 2 to view information about the current audio CD. Click on the **Update album info online** option to view any available updated details about the item.

Once an audio CD has been ripped, it is available in the **Music library** section of the Media Player app.

Music Library

The **Music library** in the **Media Player** app is the section where content that has been copied to the app can be viewed and accessed.

1 Click on this button (**Music library**) in the left-hand sidebar

2 Items in the **Music library** are displayed in the main window. In this case, the audio CD copied on the previous page is displayed in the **Music library**

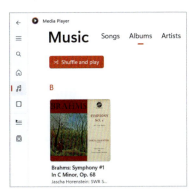

The most recently added item appears at the top of the **Music library** window.

3 Scroll down the window to view more items in the **Music library**

4 Use the buttons at the top of the **Music library** to view content according to **Songs**, **Albums**, and **Artists**

5 Use these buttons in either **Songs** or **Albums** view to sort items alphabetically or by genre

Playlists

You can create playlists containing selected songs from several albums, perhaps related to a particular theme or style.

1 Open the **Media Player** app and select **Music library** > **Albums**

2 Click an album to list the songs it contains, and select individual songs for your list

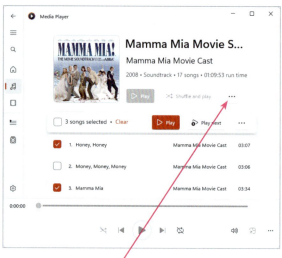

Create as many playlists as you need, to help organize the music files on your system.

3 Click the **See more** button and select **Add to** > **New playlist**

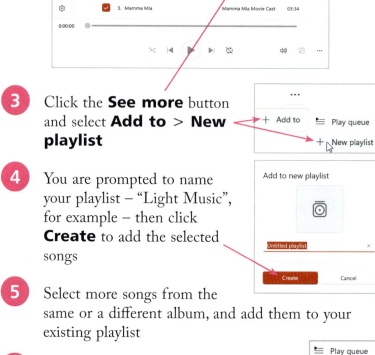

4 You are prompted to name your playlist – "Light Music", for example – then click **Create** to add the selected songs

5 Select more songs from the same or a different album, and add them to your existing playlist

6 Alternatively, choose **New playlist**, to create and name another playlist

7 To check the playlists that you have on your system, click **Playlists** on the Icon bar (or press **Ctrl + Y**)

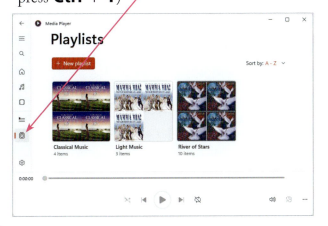

In this example, three separate playlists have been created in **Media Player**.

8 Select a playlist and click the **Play** button

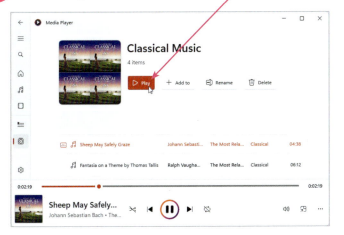

207

If you right-click the **Mini player** and select **Properties** (or press **Ctrl + I**), you will see the details of the current track – Title, Album, Track, Genre, Bit rate, File location, etc.

Properties

Title
Sheep May Safely Graze

9 With **Play** selected, the icons on the lower left of the Media Player panel are activated, and you can click the **Mini player** button (see Step 7 on page 201) or press **Ctrl + M**

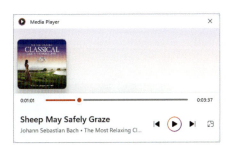

Movies & TV

Don't forget

The **Movies & TV** app may be called **Films & TV** in some regions. The items displayed will differ over time.

Hot tip

You can also add movie and TV content to your Windows 11 computer or mobile device by downloading from **YouTube**, or purchasing or renting from the Microsoft Store.

Hot tip

Click the links to see specified selections, or simply scroll the **Explore** page to see subsets of each.

1 Select the **Movies & TV** icon from the **Start** menu to start the app

Movies & TV

2 The app opens with **Explore** selected, showing featured movies. Select **Trailers** for more movies

3 Click on the **Purchased** tab to see the item that you have bought from the **Movies & TV** app, and access options for buying more

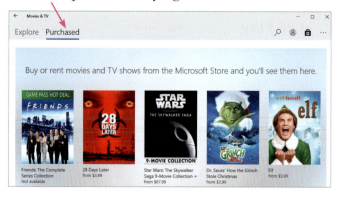

4 Click **More options (...) > Settings** to select the download quality (HD or SD)

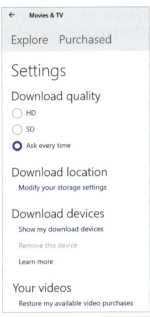

The **Movies & TV** app supports most widely used video formats, including:

.m4v .mp4
.mov .asf
.avi .wmv

5 Click the **Microsoft Store** icon to open the Store and select **Entertainment**

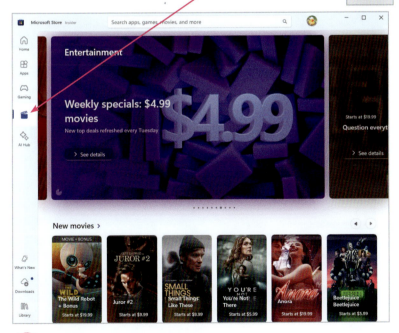

Scroll down to see selections of **New**, **Top-selling** and **Featured** movies and TV shows, and you can also search for movies by genre.

6 Review the content, and purchase and install any items that you desire

Photos App

Photos can be viewed and managed with the pre-installed **Photos** app. To use this:

1. Click on the **Photos** app from the Start menu or the Taskbar

2. The **Photos** app opens at the **Gallery** section, where all of the photos that have been added can be viewed

The Gallery section displays items in an asymmetric pattern, depending on whether photos were captured in Landscape or Portrait format.

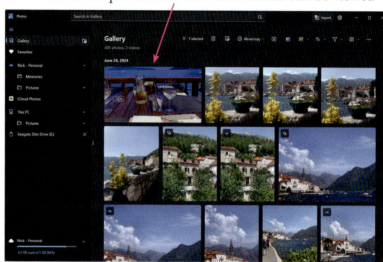

3. Double-click on a photo to view it within a new, separate, window. You can edit the photo using the options explained on page 212

4 From the Photos app homepage, use the options in the left-hand sidebar to navigate through the elements of the Photos app, including the OneDrive sections (**[Name] - Personal**) where images can be stored in this online backup service

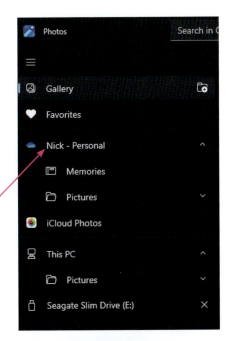

To make sure that your photos are automatically backed up, save them into the OneDrive section of the Photos app.

5 Click the **Settings** icon on the top toolbar

6 In the **Settings** section, select options for how the Photos app looks and operates

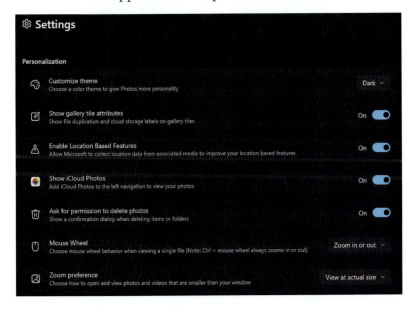

Editing Photos

You can use the **Photos** app to edit pictures. Open a picture from your collection, and the toolbar across the top offers options to handle or adjust the image.

In addition to **Edit**, the **Photos** tools include **Rotate**, **Delete**, **Print**, **Share**, and **See more (...)**.

1 Click the **Edit** button (or press **Ctrl + E**) to explore the options

If you edit an image, you can click **Save as copy**, creating a new image with the changes applied.

2 Click the **Adjustment** option on the top toolbar to access the color-editing tools

12 Networking

This chapter shows how to create a network for access to the internet, and also how to share content with other devices.

Creating a Network

You have a network when you have several devices that exchange information over a wire or over radio waves (wireless). The simplest network consists of one computer and a router that links to the internet. You can add a second computer, to share internet access and exchange information with the other computer. When the PCs are Windows 11-based, a network can help share data.

To make connections like these, your system will require components of the following types:

- Ethernet twisted-pair cables, for the wired portion.

- A router to manage the network connections.

- An internet modem, which may be integrated with the router.

- An adapter for each computer (wired or wireless).

Setting up the components

The steps you will need, and the most appropriate sequence to follow, will depend on the specific options on your system. However, the main steps will include:

- Install network adapters in the computers, where necessary (in most cases, these will be pre-installed in the computer).

- Set up or verify the internet connection – this should be provided by your Internet Service Provider (ISP).

- Configure the wireless router or access point. (This could involve installing software for the router, which may be provided on a CD or DVD. Most routers will be automatically recognized by Windows 11.)

- Start up Windows on your PC.

Windows 11 is designed to automate as much of the network setup task as possible.

Hot tip

You may already have some or all of these elements in operation if you have an existing network running a previous version of Windows.

214

Connecting to a Network

You can connect your computers to form a network using Ethernet cables and adapters or by setting up your wireless adapters and routers. When you start up each computer, Windows 11 will examine the current configuration and discover any new networks that have been established since the last startup. You can check this, or connect manually to a network, from within the **Wi-Fi** settings from the **Network & internet** section of **Settings**. To do this:

1 Open the **Settings** app and click on the **Network & internet** tab

2 With no network currently connected, drag the **Wi-Fi** button **On**

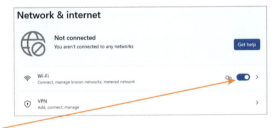

3 Click on the **Show available networks** option

4 Click on the required network

5 Click on the **Connect** button

The most common type of network for connecting to is the internet.

If your network is unavailable for any reason, this will be noted in Step 2.

...cont'd

6 Enter the password for the router to be used to connect to the Wi-Fi network

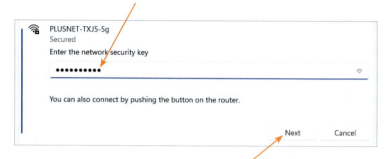

7 Click on the **Next** button

8 If the connection is successful, the network name is shown as **Connected**

9 Connected networks are shown at the top of the **Network & internet** settings window

10 Click on the **Data usage** option to see which apps are using the most data on the network

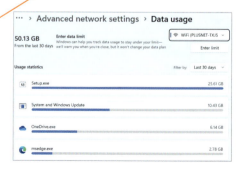

Beware

If you are using a public hotspot Wi-Fi connection, such as in a café or an airport, this may not be as secure as your home network.

Network & Internet Settings

To access the settings for creating networks and gaining access to the internet:

1 Click on the **Settings** app on the Taskbar and select **Network & internet**

2 All of the relevant network and internet options are displayed

217

When you select the **Network & internet** option, you can enable **Airplane mode** to disable wireless communication if you are on a flight where this is required.

3 Select options as required. For instance, to create a wireless network, click on the **WiFi** option

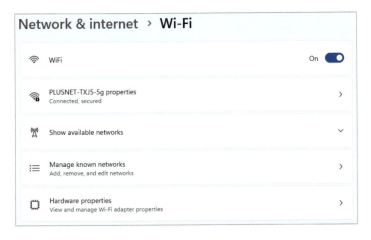

...cont'd

4 For the **Wi-Fi** option, click on a network to view its full details

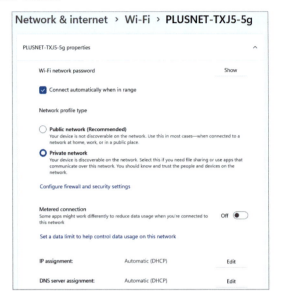

In general, you will not have to worry too much about advanced Wi-Fi and network settings unless something goes wrong and you need to give the information to your service provider.

5 Click on the **Advanced network settings** option in Step 2 on page 217 to view the more technical options for working with networks

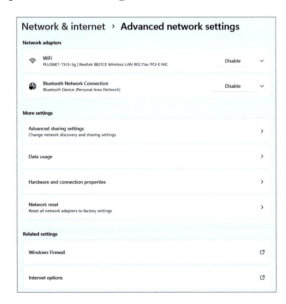

Sharing Options

If you have printers, folders, or files you want to share with other users and devices on your network:

1 Select **Settings** > **Network & internet**

2 Click on **Advanced network settings**

3 Click on the **Advanced sharing settings** option

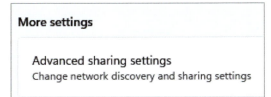

4 Drag the **File and printer sharing** button **On**, for either **Private** or **Public** networks

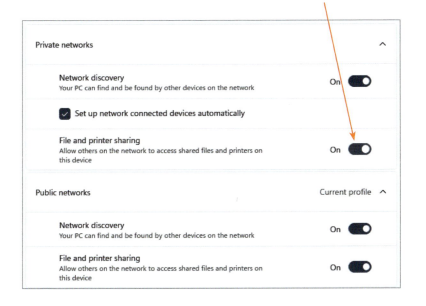

If no one else is going to be accessing your computer or printer, and you don't want to access anyone else's, then you won't have to worry about the sharing options.

If you are sharing over a network, you should be able to access the **Public** folder on another computer (providing that **Network discovery** is turned **On**). If you are the administrator of the other computer, you will also be able to access your own **Home** folder, although you will need to enter the required password for this.

...cont'd

Sharing folders and files

You can share content from your Windows 11 computer with other people.

To share folders:

1 In **File Explorer**, right-click on the folder and click on **Show more options** from the menu

2 Select **Give access to** > **Specific people...**

Give access to   >   🔒 Remove access
                                      📁 Specific people...

3 Enter the details of the person with whom you want to share the folder

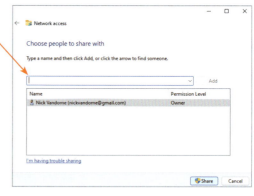

To share a file:

1 In **File Explorer**, select a file to be shared, and click on this button on the File Explorer **Menu bar**

2 Select a person with whom you want to share the file, and the method of sharing – e.g. **Mail**

Hot tip

Photos and documents can be shared directly from the **Mail** section of the **Outlook** app, by starting a new email message and clicking on the **Attach** icon to navigate to the item that you want to share.

220

Nearby Sharing

Windows 11 can also send items such as files, links, and photos to nearby PCs over Bluetooth (assuming your PC has this connectivity). To do this:

1 Select **Settings** > **System** > **Nearby sharing**

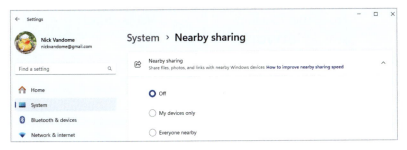

2 You can choose to share with **Everyone nearby**, or limit your sharing to **My devices only**

3 Open **File Explorer**, select a file you wish to share and click the **Share** button

4 Click the **Nearby Sharing** option to share the selected item with compatible devices

5 Check the status of **Nearby sharing** in **Quick Settings** (see page 71). Click the associated button to switch between **On** and **Off**

Beware

If **Nearby sharing** is not already enabled when you select a file to share, click on the **Turn On** button and activate it accordingly.

Mobile Hotspot

You can use the internet connection on your Windows 11 PC to allow devices to access the internet when the router is not accessible, or when you don't want to reveal your main network password, using **Mobile hotspot**.

Beware

The **Mobile hotspot** option can only be used if you are connected via Wi-Fi. It is not available if your PC is connected via an Ethernet cable.

Hot tip

Scan the QR code with the camera on a smartphone or a tablet to connect to the mobile hotspot and use the device's internet network connection.

1 Open **Settings** from the Taskbar, select **Network & internet**, then click the **Mobile hotspot** option

Mobile hotspot
Share your internet connection

2 Drag the **Mobile hotspot** button **On** to enable other devices to use the internet connection on your computer – see the Hot tip

13 Security and Maintenance

This chapter details how to get help and support for Windows 11, and also some security features.

Microsoft Support

You can review the help information offered by **Microsoft Support**.

1 Open **support.microsoft.com** and sign in to your Microsoft Account

Don't forget

Windows 11 doesn't provide the local help information found in earlier versions, but the **Microsoft Support** website has extensive help on all Microsoft products.

Hot tip

The products listed are based on your setup and on the PCs and devices associated with your Microsoft Account. Click **More Microsoft Products** in Step 1 to list others.

2 Select a product – for example, **Windows** – to see the help information that is available. Scroll down to select your version and choose one of the related topics

3 Scroll down to reveal trending topics and recent updates

4 Click on the **Resources** tab on the top toolbar and select **Community forums** to post questions, follow discussions, or share your knowledge with other users

Resources ∨

Hot tip

The topics presented will be the most currently sought after, so you can expect the list to change from time to time.

Get Help App

If you fail to find the answers you need with the usual help facilities, you can try using the **Get Help** app.

1 Select the **Get Help** entry from the **All** list

2 **Get Help** asks for details of your problem so that it can find appropriate help and support

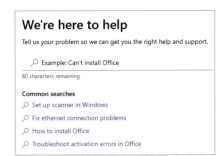

We're here to help
Tell us your problem so we can get you the right help and support.

🔎 Example: Can't install Office

80 characters remaining

Common searches
🔎 Set up scanner in Windows
🔎 Fix ethernet connection problems
🔎 How to install Office
🔎 Troubleshoot activation errors in Office

3 Enter your query – in this case, just a file type – then press **Enter** to activate a search for related information

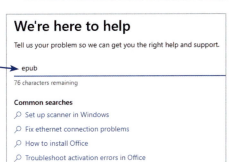

We're here to help
Tell us your problem so we can get you the right help and support.

epub

76 characters remaining

Common searches
🔎 Set up scanner in Windows
🔎 Fix ethernet connection problems
🔎 How to install Office
🔎 Troubleshoot activation errors in Office

4 The top result is displayed – in this case, reference to an app that can manage the file type mentioned in the query

File types supported for previewing files in OneDrive, SharePoint, and Teams

▸ *Applies To*

You can preview hundreds of file types in Microsoft Teams, OneDrive, and SharePoint, without installing the application used to create the file. The previews and thumbnail images appear in the web view and for customers using Files On-Demand in Windows 10.

Notes:

- For SharePoint Server Subscription Edition, preview can be shown in modern document libraries for specific file types including:
- Images: AI, BMP, EMF, EPS, GIF, JPG, JPEG, PNG, PSD, SVG, TIF, TIFF, WMF
- SharePoint page: ASPX
- If Office Online Server is installed, document preview can be shown in modern document libraries for these file types: Acrobat (PDF), PowerPoint (POTM, POTX, PPSM, PPSX, PPT, PPTM, PPTX), Rich Text (RTF), Word (DOC, DOCM, DOCX, DOTM, DOTX).

5 Select the **Learn More** link to see full details of the response

You must be connected to the internet to use the **Get Help** app, and it is recommended that you are signed in with your Microsoft Account.

A plain language outline of your problem is best, since it will be matched against queries that other users have submitted.

225

If the articles suggested don't resolve your query, click the **Contact Support** button.

Contact Support

Windows Security

The **Windows Security** app, which is pre-installed with Windows 11, can be used to give a certain amount of protection against viruses and malicious software. To use it:

1 Select **Settings** > **Privacy & security**

2 Click on the **Windows Security** option

3 The **Windows Security** section contains the main categories for helping to keep your Windows 11 computer safe and secure

4 Click on the **Open Windows Security** button

5 The options in Step 3 can be selected in the **Windows Security** section

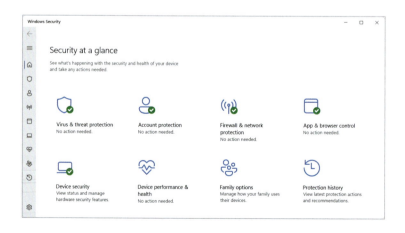

Windows Security provides protection against malicious software such as viruses and spyware, so you do not have to install separate utilities.

6 Click on the **Virus & threat protection** option to see details of the last virus checks and the status of protection updates

Virus & threat protection
No action needed.

7 Click on the **Quick scan** button to run a check of your system

○ Virus & threat protection

Protection for your device against threats.

🔄 **Current threats**

No current threats.
Last scan: 12/20/2024 1:01 PM (quick scan)
0 threat(s) found.
Scan lasted 37 seconds
27887 files scanned.

Quick scan

Scan options

Allowed threats

Protection history

○ Virus & threat protection

Protection for your device against threats.

🔄 **Current threats**

Quick scan running...
Estimated time remaining: 00:00:52
680 files scanned

Cancel

Feel free to keep working while we scan your device.

Windows Security also alerts you when spyware attempts to install or run, or when apps try to change important Windows settings.

227

8 Once a quick scan has been completed, click on the **Scan options** link to access options to do more scans. Check on one of the options – e.g. **Full scan** – and click on the **Scan now** button to perform the selected scan

Scan options

Run a scan from the available options on this page.

No current threats.
Last scan: 12/22/2024 11:58 AM (quick scan)
0 threat(s) found.
Scan lasted 38 seconds
12261 files scanned.

Allowed threats

Protection history

○ Quick scan

Checks folders in your system where threats are commonly found.

● Full scan

Checks all files and running programs on your hard disk. This scan could take longer than one hour.

○ Custom scan

Choose which files and locations you want to check.

○ Microsoft Defender Antivirus (offline scan)

Some malicious software can be particularly difficult to remove from your device. Microsoft Defender Antivirus (offline scan) can help find and remove them using up-to-date threat definitions. This will restart your device and will take about 15 minutes.

Scan now

...cont'd

9 Click on the **Account protection** option to apply security settings and options for your own Microsoft Account

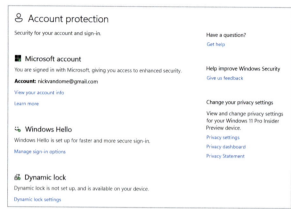

10 Click on the **Device performance & health** option to view a report about the overall health of your computer

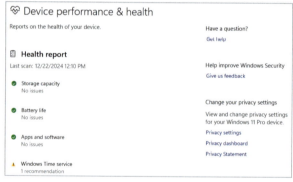

11 Click on the **Family options** option to apply parental controls for children using your computer

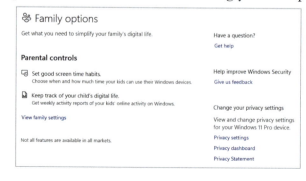

Hot tip

Parental controls can be set for items such as restricting access to certain types of websites and setting time limits for using a Windows 11 device.

12 Click on the **App & browser control** option to apply security settings for apps on your computer to protect it against unwanted apps, files, and websites

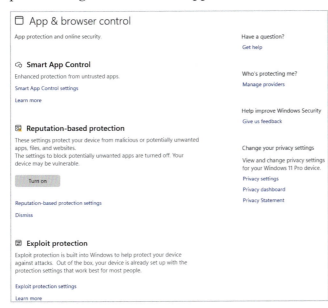

13 Click on the **Device security** option to view some of the built-in security options for your Windows 11 computer

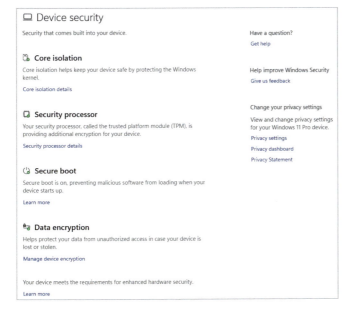

The **Device security** options do not usually require any action, but they detail some of the more technical security features on your computer.

Windows Firewall

Within the **Windows Security** options is an important feature for using the built-in firewall, to help prevent malicious software from entering your computer from the internet, via your router. To use this:

Don't forget

Microsoft Defender Firewall is **On** by default in Windows 11, but you can turn it **Off** if you have another firewall installed and active.

1 Open the **Windows Security** panel, as shown on page 226, and select **Firewall & network protection**

Firewall & network protection
No action needed.

2 Select one of the options – e.g. **Private network** – to view the firewall settings for this item (by default, the firewall should be **On**)

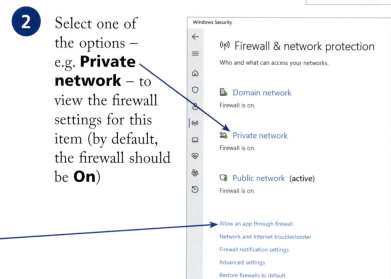

Hot tip

Click **Allow an app through firewall** in Step 2 to view a list of allowed apps that can communicate through **Windows Defender Firewall**. Select apps to be allowed through the firewall, as required.

230

3 The firewall settings for the selected item are displayed. By default, **Microsoft Defender Firewall** should be **On**. If it is **Off**, click on it to turn the firewall **On**

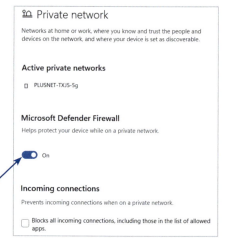

Windows Update

To view the status of Windows updates on your system:

1 Open **Settings** > **Windows Update**

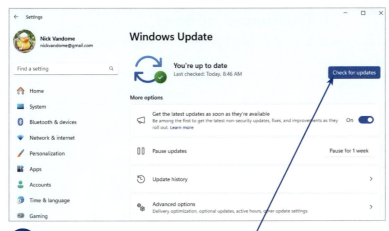

In Windows 11, **Windows Update** updates can be paused for up to a week at a time, but they will eventually be installed.

2 Click on the **Check for updates** button, or select **Update history** to view installed updates

3 To instruct **Windows Update** when to apply updates, select **Advanced options** > **Active hours**

4 Click on the **Adjust active hours** option and select **Manually** or **Automatically**

5 For the **Manually** option above, select a **Start time** or **End time** and scroll to select a time

Windows 11 updates are provided on a regular basis for fixes, with major updates usually provided annually.

...cont'd

You can apply controls to the way Windows installs updates. To make changes:

1 Open **Settings** > **Windows Update**, then select **Advanced options**

If you are using a metered connection (where charges may apply), updates won't normally be downloaded.

- Get updates to other Microsoft products when you update Windows.
- You can choose to restart to finish applying updates, even during active hours or over metered connections.
- See notification messages when restarts are scheduled for your system.
- You may be offered optional updates for features, quality, or drivers.

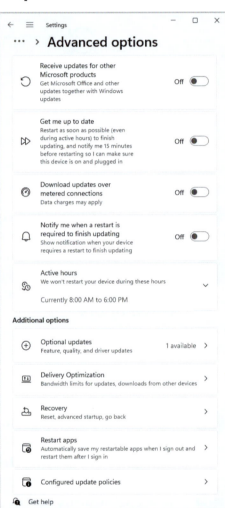

Recovery

If you are having problems with your PC, you can select **Recovery** from the **Additional options** section of **Advanced options**. From here, you have these options: **Reset this PC** (reinstalling Windows), **Go back** (uninstalling the latest update), or **Advanced startup** (changing your startup settings).

Index

Symbols

A

B

235